daybook, *n.* a book in which the events of the day are recorded; *specif.* a journal or diary

DAYBOOK
of Critical Reading and Writing

AUTHOR

VICKI SPANDEL

CONSULTING AUTHORS

RUTH NATHAN

LAURA ROBB

Great Source Education Group
a Houghton Mifflin Company
Wilmington, Massachusetts

Consulting Authors

Vicki Spandel, director of Write Traits, provides training to writing teachers both nationally and internationally. A former teacher and journalist, Vicki is the author of more than twenty books, including the new third edition of *Creating Writers* and the Write Traits Classroom Kits®.

Ruth Nathan, one of the authors of *Writers Express* and *Write Away,* is the author of many professional books and articles on literacy. She currently teaches in third grade as well as consults with numerous schools and organizations on reading.

Laura Robb, author of *Teaching Reading in Middle School; Teaching Reading in Social Studies, Science, and Math;* and *Literacy Links: The Emergent Literacy At-Risk Children Need* has taught language arts at Powhatan School in Boyce, Virginia, for more than thirty-five years. She also mentors and coaches teachers in Virginia public schools and speaks at conferences throughout the country.

Book Design: Christine Ronan and Sean O'Neill, Ronan Design

Developed by Nieman, Inc.

Printed in the United States of America

International Standard Book Number: 0-669-50099-2
1 2 3 4 5 6 7 8 9 10 – POO – 09 08 07 06 05 04 03

Readers

Great Source wishes to acknowledge the many insights and improvements made to the Daybooks *thanks to the work of the following teachers and educators.*

Ellen Barker
Patronis Elementary School
Panama City Beach, Florida

Linda Beitzel
Butterfield School
Libertyville, Illinois

Suzanne Bennett
Patronis Elementary School
Panama City Beach, Florida

Kathy Carson
Swasey Central School
Brentwood, New Hampshire

Lisa Conner
Arrowhead Elementary School
Aurora, Colorado

Janel deBoer
Stonewall Magnet School
Lexington, Kentucky

Neva Fleckenstein
Rohnert Park, California

Kelly Forehand
Patronis Elementary School
Panama City Beach, Florida

Kim Freed
Sagebrush Elementary School
Aurora, Colorado

Jean Fullerton
Dike-Newell School
Bath, Maine

Olivia Gonzalez
93rd St. School
Los Angeles, California

Rosemarie Granger
Fisher Mitchell School
Bath, Maine

Sharon Kroll
Culver City, California

Lorena La Rosa
Wesley Matthews Elementary
   School
Miami, Florida

Laura Lewis
Patronis Elementary School
Panama City Beach, Florida

Deb Love
Wanamaker Elementary School
Topeka, Kansas

Susan Neff
Berryton Elementary School
Berryton, Kansas

Lillian Pirog
North Londonderry School
Londonderry, New Hampshire

Julie Proctor
Swasey Central School
Brentwood, New Hampshire

Beth Schmar
Emporia State University
Emporia, Kansas

Lori Sizelove
Adler Park School
Libertyville, Illinois

Debbie Tofflemire
West Indianola Elementary
West Indianola, Kansas

Carolyne von Schmidt
Littleton High School
Littleton, Colorado

Kelly Wessel
Oak Knoll School
Cary, Illinois

Kelly Wince
Apple Pie Ridge Elementary
Winchester, Virginia

Table of Contents

Table of Contents

Pupil's Skills and Strategies

LESSON TITLE	LITERATURE	AUTHOR	RESPONSE STRATEGY
Unit 1: Reading Stories			
Character Clues	"Growing Up" from *More Tales of Amanda Pig*	Jean Van Leeuwen	underline
Where Are We?	from *Henry and Mudge Under the Yellow Moon*	Cynthia Rylant	circle words
What Is Happening?	"The Scary Movie" from *The Adventures of Sugar and Junior*	Angela Shelf Medearis	ask questions
Unit 2: Reading Nonfiction			
Looking for the Main Idea	from *The Sun Is Always Shining Somewhere*	Allan Fowler	mark up the text (clarify)
Big Ideas and Small	from *Germs Make Me Sick!*	Melvin Berger	mark up the text (clarify)
What's It About?	from *Sleep Is for Everyone*	Paul Showers	retell
Unit 3: Reading Authors			
Learning About Characters	from *Jamal's Busy Day*	Wade Hudson	ask questions
Authors Choose Words	from *Truman's Aunt Farm*	Jama Kim Rattigan	circle words
What a Problem!	from "The Wishing Well"	Arnold Lobel	visualize

CRITICAL READING SKILL	WRITING	FOCUS STATEMENT
character	character sketch	You can learn about characters by what they say or do.
setting	setting	The place where a story happens is called the setting.
plot	describe beginning, middle, and end	Plot is what happens in the beginning, middle, and end of a story.
main idea	describe the main idea	When you read nonfiction, look for the main idea and for details.
main idea and details	write about main idea and details	Details tell about the main idea.
message of the story	retell a story	When you read, you try to understand what the author is saying.
character	character sketch	Writers make a character seem real.
word choice	letter	Writers choose words to express themselves.
plot	book cover showing story's problem	Stories often show a problem and how it is solved.

CRITICAL READING SKILL	WRITING	FOCUS STATEMENT
rhyme	write rhymes	When sounds repeat at the end of a line of poetry, they rhyme.
feeling in poetry	poem	Poets use words and sounds to show feeling.
word choice in poetry	poem	Poets pick their words so that you can "see" their ideas.
retell	summarize, and note details	As you read, ask yourself, "What is this writer trying to teach me?"
sequencing	retell the sequence	As you read, note the order in which things happen.
topic	retell	The subject of a piece of writing is called a topic.
problem	write a story	Usually the characters in a story have a problem.
connect	book review	As you read, ask yourself, "How is this story like something I know?"
message of the story	write a story	As you read, ask yourself what the author might be trying to tell you.

Correlation to Write Away, © 2002

Daybook Lesson	Writing Activity	*Write Away* ©2002
Reading Stories		
1. Character Clues	write a character sketch (sentences)	50–55
2. Where Are We?	write a setting sketch (sentences)	50–55
3. What Is Happening?	write a story with three parts	39
Reading Nonfiction		
1. Looking for the Main Idea	summarize main idea (paragraph)	56–63
2. Big Ideas and Small	summarize main idea (paragraph)	56–63
3. What's It About?	retell (paragraph)	56–63
Reading Authors		
1. Learning About Characters	write a character sketch (sentences)	50–55
2. Authors Choose Words	write a friendly letter	72–75
3. What a Problem!	draw a book cover	49

O v e r v i e w

Purpose

What is a *Daybook*? Why do I need one? How do I use it? These questions come up almost immediately among teachers when they first see a *Daybook*.

A *Daybook* is a keepable journal-like book designed to improve students' reading and writing. Its purpose is to engage students in brief, integrated reading and writing activities daily or at least weekly. By asking students regularly to read good literature and write about it, students will become better readers and writers.

Lessons

Each lesson is a brief, highly focused activity that concentrates on one aspect of critical reading. By focusing on a single skill, students can see how to do critical reading. The lessons include models showing how to respond actively to literature in the Response Notes. Each *Daybook* even begins with an introductory "Active Reading" unit to show students some of the ways to response actively to literature. Then, in the lessons, students respond creatively to the literature through writing descriptions, journal entries, narrative paragraphs, and many other kinds of writing—all in response to great literature.

Literature

The literature included in this *Daybook* came from suggestions teachers made. More than twenty master teachers recommended their favorite books and authors, and from these came the quality selections included here. Each selection was reviewed for its appropriateness and for its illustration of the critical reading skill at the heart of the lesson. In addition, a blend of traditional and non-traditional authors, fiction and nonfiction, and different genres was considered. At each step, teachers from the appropriate grade level commented upon the literature, readability, appropriateness of the activities, and critical reading skill.

Goals

The final result can be seen in the *Daybook*, where each individual lesson has been crafted to fit in the reading and writing curricula of elementary teachers. The goals of the *Daybook* are reflected in the headings of the units:
- to teach students how to read actively
- to build the essential skills (such as finding the main idea) for reading well
- to develop an appreciation for the elements of fiction, poetry, and nonfiction
- to create a love and appreciation of language
- to introduce students to and foster an appreciation of fine authors and great literature

Uses for Daybooks

Teachers suggested numerous ways to use the *Daybook*, from introducing author studies to reinforcing key reading and writing skills. It can serve as a portfolio of daily reading and writing practice or as a guide to introducing key skills. How you use the *Daybook* ultimately depends upon you. The *Daybook* can become for you a powerful tool to help create better, more confident readers and writers.

Who Is This Book For?

The immediate response to the question "Who is this book for?" is that the audience is normal, ordinary students. The *Daybook* targets everyday students in grade 2—neither the best nor the worst, just average students.

What's Average?

The question about the audience for the *Daybook* comes up when considering how the literature was chosen, how its readability was gauged, what assignments were chosen, and how much readiness or scaffolding is needed in each lesson. But even average students vary widely and respond much differently to individual lessons.

For example, in this *Daybook*, students read a selection from *Too Many Tamales* by Gary Soto. For students in areas without exposure to Mexican cuisine, tamales will not be familiar food. Teachers in those areas will need to explain the food to them. In one state, students may be tested on writing descriptive paragraphs in the state assessment exams and thus practice writing descriptions regularly; but, in another state, descriptive paragraphs may have just been introduced. To establish what would work on average, then, state standards as well as the appropriate on-grade-level texts were referenced. (Writing assignments, for example, were matched to expectations in appropriate grade-level texts such as *Write Away*, as were the reading skills addressed.) Current practices and materials, in other words, provided reference points to check assumptions about what's average.

Why Use These Authors?

Likewise, selecting specific authors to feature at grade 2 seems on the surface somewhat arbitrary. Here teachers guided the selection of which literature and which authors to use. Asking twenty master teachers to recommend literature and authors hardly approaches anything close to scientific reliability, but it served as a useful touchstone. The intent is not to limit authors or a piece of literature to a specific grade level as much as it is to offer a rich, wide variety of literature at each grade level.

What's the Readability?

For students in the elementary grades, helping students find materials at their specific reading level is a major challenge. Each student is different, and the right reading level for one student poses insuperable challenges for the next student. The readability of selections in the *Daybook* will change from lesson to lesson. The entire notion of "readability level" depends, among other elements, on word choice, sentence length and complexity, and subject matter. Readability can vary from student to student. So, it quickly becomes apparent that one *Daybook* can hardly be a perfect fit for all students.

If one selection seems too easy or too hard for your students, realize that the selections and "readability" change throughout the *Daybook*. Lessons are organized by the critical reading skills taught, not by the level of the selection.

How Will I Know If I Should Use the *Daybook*?

Is this *Daybook* right for my students? As teachers, you routinely ask this question—about the *Daybook* and all of the other books in your classroom. You want assurance that the selections will match the reading abilities of your students. One obvious answer is simply to try some lessons with your students. The experience of other teachers has been that those who get started and work through some lessons with students find a way to make the crucial fit between the materials and the students. Each lesson in this teacher's guide includes a **Vocabulary Activity** and a **Prereading Activity** to improve students' readiness for the selection. Supporting activities such as the Vocabulary blackline master for each selection will help create readiness with more challenging selections.

In the end, the best guide will be your own experience and instincts as a teacher. Try a number of lessons with students. Encourage them, challenge them, and evaluate them. Let your students be your guide in deciding whether or not the *Daybook* helps and challenges them.

How to Use the Daybook

The *Daybook* is a tool. Like any tool, such as a hammer or screwdriver, the *Daybook* can have one purpose or many, depending on the ingenuity of the user. Teachers who reviewed the *Daybook* lessons suggested any number of ways they would use them.

1. In the Reading Period

Reviewers of the *Daybook*s often introduced *Daybook* lessons to students during part of their reading period. Whether they were using thematically linked trade books or anthologies, teachers saw the *Daybook*s' focused lessons as helpful ways to reinforce (or introduce) key skills and bring more good literature into their classrooms.

Daybooks also served as ways to kick off author studies or a series of reading skills lessons. Other teachers preferred to introduce an author or a skill, such as prediction, on their own and then complement their lessons with ones from the *Daybook*.

2. In the Language Arts Period

Because each lesson begins with great literature, teachers liked launching writing activities with *Daybook* lessons. Each lesson gives students literature to which they respond as well as a series of scaffolded assignments to help students get ready to write. Because the *Daybook* includes so many strong writing assignments (summaries, descriptive paragraphs, narrative paragraphs, journal entries, and so on), teachers like the clear, efficient ways the *Daybook* motivated students to write. The daily writing in the *Daybook*s appealed to many reviewers facing state tests, because their students would be able to practice regularly and build confidence as writers before test day.

3. In Reading and Writing Workshops

Numerous teachers use reading and writing workshops each week in their classrooms, and they found the integrated nature of the *Daybook* lessons to be a perfect fit for what they were trying to accomplish. The goals of their workshops and the *Daybook* lessons matched up almost exactly. Each lesson leads students from literature directly into writing, helping students to see the connections between what they read and what they write.

4. In Alternative Settings

As after-school tutorials and summer sessions become more common, teachers are looking for ways to reinforce key reading and writing skills. The brief, efficient lessons in the *Daybook*s fit well with the brief sessions in after-school and summer school programs. Teachers also pick and choose among the lessons in these alternative settings, focusing on areas where students need the greatest help. Here the flexibility of individual lessons that integrate reading and writing becomes valuable, because each lesson weaves together so many elements: fine literature, active reading, critical reading skills, and creative writing.

The uses of the *Daybook*s are limited only by the teachers using them. But, however you choose to use them, keep in mind that the original intent behind the *Daybook*s was to create a flexible tool for teachers to help them give students meaningful reading and writing activities, day after day, in their classrooms.

F r e q u e n t l y   A s k e d   Q u e s t i o n s

Reviewers raised a number of questions during the development of the *Daybook* manuscript that might be useful to teachers using the series for the first time.

1. Why is it called a *Daybook*?

A *Daybook* traditionally is "a book in which daily transactions are recorded," but nowadays it is being used to mean "a journal." The name connotes "daily work," which is the intent behind the *Daybook*, as well as the idea of "journal," because a *Daybook* does become a place where students can record their work and ideas.

2. Can students write in the *Daybooks*?

Absolutely! In fact, that is the purpose behind this format. By writing in the book—their book— students begin to "own" the book. It records their work and their ideas. It becomes a personal record of their creative efforts, a portfolio of sorts of their development as readers and writers. One of the strongest elements of the *Daybook*s comes in allowing students to mark in the text, highlighting, underscoring, circling, and writing notes. Reading and writing in the same book creates the seamless integration that makes the *Daybook* work.

3. Can I photocopy these pages?

No, photocopying the pages in the *Daybook* pupil's book is prohibited. It violates copyright laws that protect the authors' rights to their work and the publishers' rights to the product. Besides, the effect of working on a few loose-leaf sheets of paper or of working in a *Daybook* of one's own is very different. So, not only is copying unlawful, but it fails as a teaching practice.

4. Can I skip around, picking and choosing the lessons?

Yes, you can pick and choose the lessons you want to teach. One strong feature of the *Daybook* is its incredible flexibility, making it a perfect tool for teachers who want to interweave *Daybook* lessons into a crowded language arts or reading class period. The lessons in the *Daybook* have been organized into units with a logic and continuity that make sense; but other organizations of the lessons may well fit better with the specific needs of your classroom, and you should feel free to take advantage of the flexibility in the *Daybook's* lessons.

5. What if my students are not active readers and need more help in learning how to mark up a text?

Begin with the Active Reading unit that introduces students to the most common ways of marking up a text. That's the obvious starting point, but it's only a start. Not every child will, in a few quick lessons, "get it." That's what the *Daybook* is for. Through repeated practice, students will "get it" through repeated practice and learn how to become active readers.

6. How were the literature selections chosen?

First, we asked approximately twenty master teachers what sort of literature they wanted to see, and they listed their favorite authors. With that background, the individual selections were evaluated on several criteria—the authors, interest and accessibility of the selection, fit with the critical reading skill and writing skill, and overall balance of genre, sex, race, and ethnicity. But, first and foremost, the mandate from reviewers was good literature by good authors, and that ultimately guided selection of every piece.

7. How do I assess students' work?

Assessment looms as an issue for almost any classroom practice, including the use of *Daybook*s. How you "grade" them is an individual decision. Most teachers who have used *Daybook*s at the upper grades collect them periodically and mark in them. They may make an encouraging comment, check off that work was completed, and acknowledge the hard work and creativity students have poured into their *Daybook*s. The important issue is that you assess students as active readers *and* as writers and that you take into account that students' writings in the *Daybook*s are responses to literature more than finished, published compositions.

Organization of the Daybooks

The units and lessons in the *Daybooks* follow a simple organization designed to offer you the greatest flexibility in using the book.

Unit Organization

Throughout the *Daybooks*, three or four lessons are organized into a unit. This gives you a concentration of lessons on a general idea, such as Reading Fiction, allowing the introduction of all of the key skills (plot, setting, characters) at one time. The units are focused on broad areas:

Introduction: Active Reading
- introduces the fundamentals of marking up texts, such as highlighting, underlining, questioning, predicting, and visualizing

Reading Stories
- looks at basic reading skills, such as understanding character, setting, and plot

Reading Nonfiction
- focuses on reading elements related to genre, such as topic, main idea, characters, and so forth

Reading Poetry
- highlights appreciation of poetry, such as rhymes, sensory images, and so on

Reading Authors
- studies of individual authors, their ideas, and skills related to their fiction

Overview

The table of contents provides an overview of different components of the book, including:
- critical reading skills
- literature titles
- authors
- genres, organized by unit.

Focus/Strategy   Lesson

Author
Literature

TABLE OF CONTENTS

Unit Title

UNIT 2

Reading Nonfiction   PAGES **29–40**

main idea   1. Looking for the   **Allan Fowler**   **30** ····· Author
                 Main Idea   from *The Sun Is Always*
                                          Shining Somewhere (NONFICTION)

Lesson Title

main idea/   2. Big Ideas and Small   **Melvin Berger**   **34**
details   from *Germs Make Me Sick!* ····· Literature
                                          (NONFICTION)

retelling   3. What's It About?   **Paul Showers**   **38**
                                          from *Sleep Is for Everyone*

Critical Reading Skill   (NONFICTION)

UNIT 3

Reading Authors   PAGES **41–58**

characters   1. Learning About   **Wade Hudson**   **42**
                  Characters   from *Jamal's Busy Day*
                                          (FICTION)

word choice   2. Authors Choose   **Jama Kim Rattigan**   **47**
                  Words   from *Truman's Aunt Farm*
                                          (FICTION)

plot   3. What a Problem!   **Arnold Lobel**   **53**
                                          from *"The Wishing Well"*
                                          (FICTION)

4

Lesson Organization

Each lesson also follows a simple, flexible organization. A typical lesson begins with a few sentences that introduce a critical reading skill. Just before reading the selection, the lesson gives the response strategy that tells students what to look for and how to mark up the text in the Response Notes as active readers. The "response" strategies given here pick up the active reading strategies introduced in the first unit, Introduction: Active Reading.

The literature selection follows, after which—in most cases—students have an initial activity that invites them simply to respond to the selection.

Focus on Critical Reading

Lesson Title

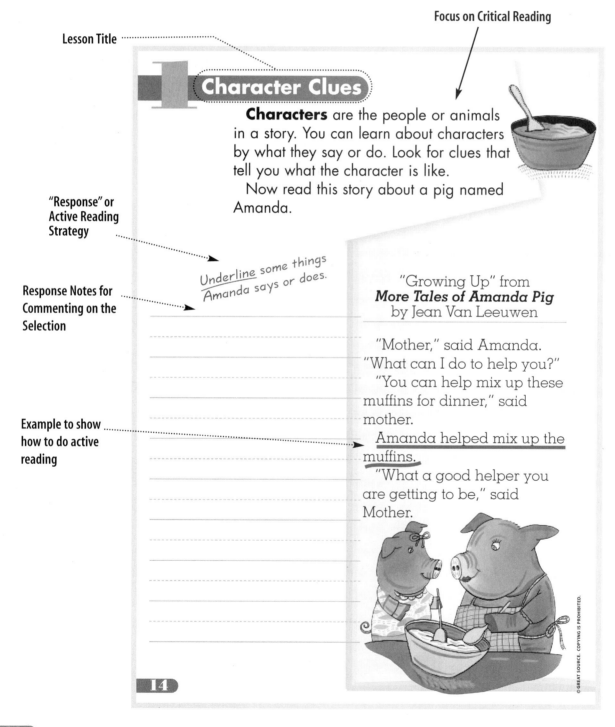

Character Clues

Characters are the people or animals in a story. You can learn about characters by what they say or do. Look for clues that tell you what the character is like.

Now read this story about a pig named Amanda.

"Response" or Active Reading Strategy

Underline some things Amanda says or does.

Response Notes for Commenting on the Selection

"Growing Up" from
More Tales of Amanda Pig
by Jean Van Leeuwen

"Mother," said Amanda. "What can I do to help you?"
"You can help mix up these muffins for dinner," said mother.
<u>Amanda helped mix up the muffins.</u>
"What a good helper you are getting to be," said Mother.

Example to show how to do active reading

14

An initial activity asks for students' thoughts, feelings, or first impressions of the selection. Then one or more activities prepares students to write a longer assignment.

Structured Activity on Selection

Running Head with Unit Title

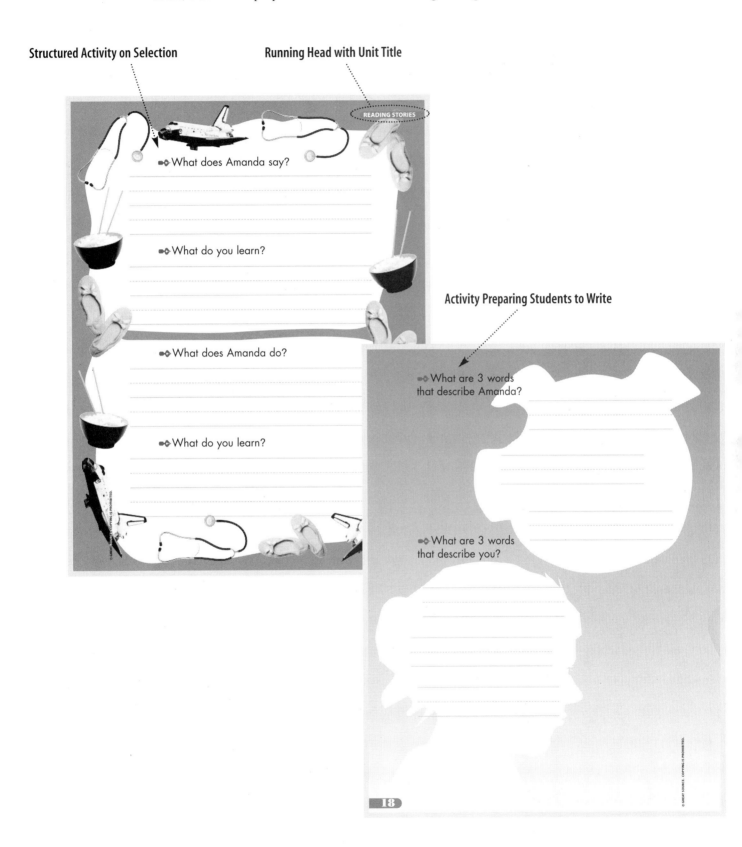

READING STORIES

➥❖ What does Amanda say?

➥❖ What do you learn?

➥❖ What does Amanda do?

➥❖ What do you learn?

Activity Preparing Students to Write

➥❖ What are 3 words that describe Amanda?

➥❖ What are 3 words that describe you?

18

The last writing activity culminates the lesson and asks for a writing product, such as a descriptive paragraph, summary, review, character sketch, or the like. The lesson then ends with a summary statement that restates the critical reading idea.

Culminating Writing Activity

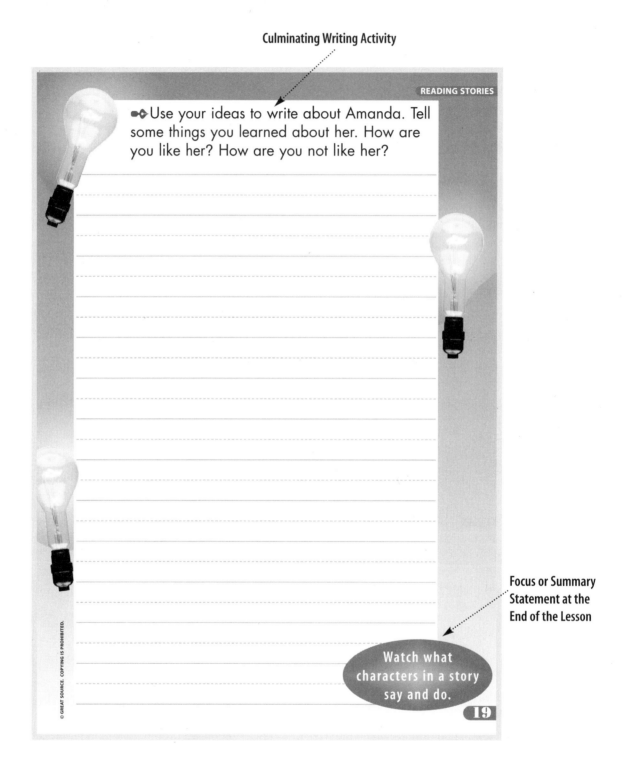

READING STORIES

Use your ideas to write about Amanda. Tell some things you learned about her. How are you like her? How are you not like her?

Focus or Summary Statement at the End of the Lesson

Watch what characters in a story say and do.

19

Teacher's Guide Organization

Each lesson in the *Teacher's Guide* helps briefly to prepare students for the selection, introducing new or difficult words, providing prereading strategies, and listing additional reading selections.

To guide students through the selection, each lesson plan discusses the response strategy and critical reading skill found in the pupil's edition.

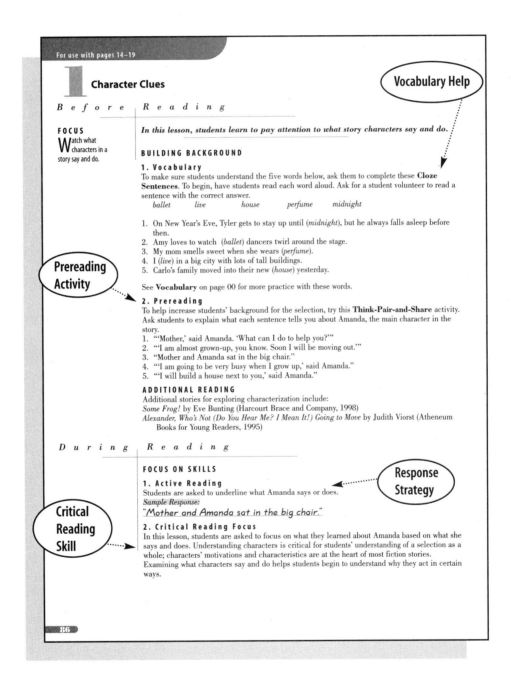

For use with pages 14–19

1 Character Clues

Vocabulary Help

Before Reading

FOCUS
Watch what characters in a story say and do.

In this lesson, students learn to pay attention to what story characters say and do.

BUILDING BACKGROUND

1. Vocabulary
To make sure students understand the five words below, ask them to complete these **Cloze Sentences**. To begin, have students read each word aloud. Ask for a student volunteer to read a sentence with the correct answer.

    ballet   live   house   perfume   midnight

1. On New Year's Eve, Tyler gets to stay up until (*midnight*), but he always falls asleep before then.
2. Amy loves to watch (*ballet*) dancers twirl around the stage.
3. My mom smells sweet when she wears (*perfume*).
4. I (*live*) in a big city with lots of tall buildings.
5. Carlo's family moved into their new (*house*) yesterday.

See **Vocabulary** on page 00 for more practice with these words.

Prereading Activity

2. Prereading
To help increase students' background for the selection, try this **Think-Pair-and-Share** activity. Ask students to explain what each sentence tells you about Amanda, the main character in the story.
1. "'Mother,' said Amanda. 'What can I do to help you?'"
2. "'I am almost grown-up, you know. Soon I will be moving out.'"
3. "Mother and Amanda sat in the big chair."
4. "'I am going to be very busy when I grow up,' said Amanda."
5. "'I will build a house next to you,' said Amanda."

ADDITIONAL READING
Additional stories for exploring characterization include:
Some Frog! by Eve Bunting (Harcourt Brace and Company, 1998)
Alexander, Who's Not (Do You Hear Me? I Mean It!) Going to Move by Judith Viorst (Atheneum Books for Young Readers, 1995)

During Reading

FOCUS ON SKILLS

1. Active Reading
Students are asked to underline what Amanda says or does.
Sample Response:
"Mother and Amanda sat in the big chair."

Response Strategy

Critical Reading Skill

2. Critical Reading Focus
In this lesson, students are asked to focus on what they learned about Amanda based on what she says and does. Understanding characters is critical for students' understanding of a selection as a whole; characters' motivations and characteristics are at the heart of most fiction stories. Examining what characters say and do helps students begin to understand why they act in certain ways.

86

To help teach the critical reading skill in the lesson, key excerpts from the selection are presented for teachers to launch a class discussion.

Suggested classroom questions appear beside annotated excerpts. These represent the sorts of questions that point out where in the selection the critical reading focus is most clearly shown. This page also contains suggested discussion topics to help students comprehend the reading.

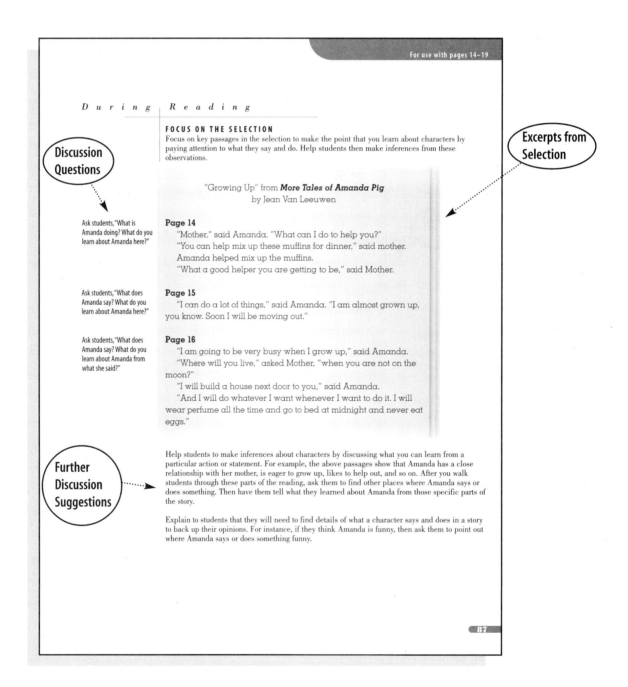

For use with pages 14–19

During Reading

FOCUS ON THE SELECTION
Focus on key passages in the selection to make the point that you learn about characters by paying attention to what they say and do. Help students then make inferences from these observations.

Discussion Questions

Excerpts from Selection

"Growing Up" from *More Tales of Amanda Pig*
by Jean Van Leeuwen

Ask students, "What is Amanda doing? What do you learn about Amanda here?"

Page 14
"Mother," said Amanda. "What can I do to help you?"
"You can help mix up these muffins for dinner," said mother.
Amanda helped mix up the muffins.
"What a good helper you are getting to be," said Mother.

Ask students, "What does Amanda say? What do you learn about Amanda here?"

Page 15
"I can do a lot of things," said Amanda. "I am almost grown up, you know. Soon I will be moving out."

Ask students, "What does Amanda say? What do you learn about Amanda from what she said?"

Page 16
"I am going to be very busy when I grow up," said Amanda.
"Where will you live," asked Mother, "when you are not on the moon?"
"I will build a house next door to you," said Amanda.
"And I will do whatever I want whenever I want to do it. I will wear perfume all the time and go to bed at midnight and never eat eggs."

Further Discussion Suggestions

Help students to make inferences about characters by discussing what you can learn from a particular action or statement. For example, the above passages show that Amanda has a close relationship with her mother, is eager to grow up, likes to help out, and so on. After you walk students through these parts of the reading, ask them to find other places where Amanda says or does something. Then have them tell what they learned about Amanda from those specific parts of the story.

Explain to students that they will need to find details of what a character says and does in a story to back up their opinions. For instance, if they think Amanda is funny, then ask them to point out where Amanda says or does something funny.

87

After reading, students will be able to answer comprehension questions. They will also be ready for rereading the selection and completing the writing activity. The *Teacher's Guide* lesson provides After Reading questions, a rereading suggestion, and sample responses to the writing activities. It also lists writing reminders that students can use when checking their work and includes a brief checklist for teacher assessment.

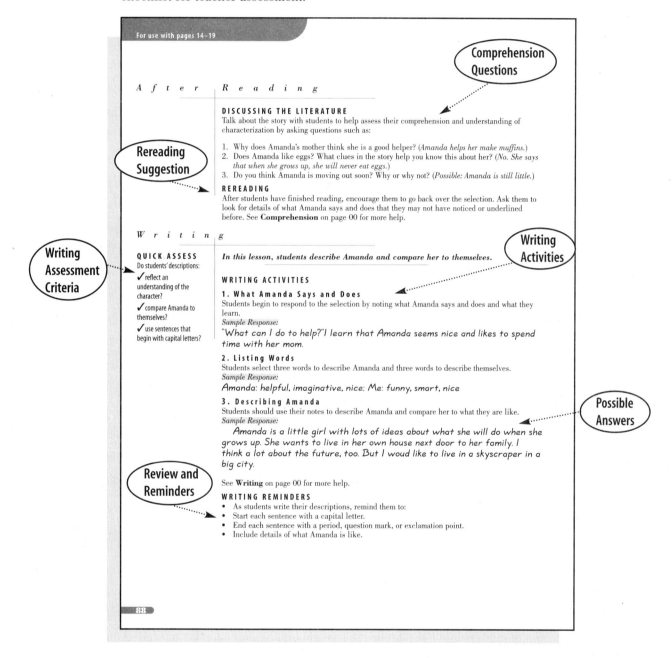

For use with pages 14–19

Comprehension Questions

A f t e r R e a d i n g

DISCUSSING THE LITERATURE
Talk about the story with students to help assess their comprehension and understanding of characterization by asking questions such as:

1. Why does Amanda's mother think she is a good helper? (*Amanda helps her make muffins.*)
2. Does Amanda like eggs? What clues in the story help you know this about her? (*No. She says that when she grows up, she will never eat eggs.*)
3. Do you think Amanda is moving out soon? Why or why not? (*Possible: Amanda is still little.*)

Rereading Suggestion

REREADING
After students have finished reading, encourage them to go back over the selection. Ask them to look for details of what Amanda says and does that they may not have noticed or underlined before. See **Comprehension** on page 00 for more help.

W r i t i n g

Writing Activities

Writing Assessment Criteria

QUICK ASSESS
Do students' descriptions:
✓ reflect an understanding of the character?
✓ compare Amanda to themselves?
✓ use sentences that begin with capital letters?

In this lesson, students describe Amanda and compare her to themselves.

WRITING ACTIVITIES

1. What Amanda Says and Does
Students begin to respond to the selection by noting what Amanda says and does and what they learn.
Sample Response:
"What can I do to help?" I learn that Amanda seems nice and likes to spend time with her mom.

2. Listing Words
Students select three words to describe Amanda and three words to describe themselves.
Sample Response:
Amanda: helpful, imaginative, nice; Me: funny, smart, nice

3. Describing Amanda
Students should use their notes to describe Amanda and compare her to what they are like.
Sample Response:
Amanda is a little girl with lots of ideas about what she will do when she grows up. She wants to live in her own house next door to her family. I think a lot about the future, too. But I woud like to live in a skyscraper in a big city.

Possible Answers

See **Writing** on page 00 for more help.

Review and Reminders

WRITING REMINDERS
• As students write their descriptions, remind them to:
• Start each sentence with a capital letter.
• End each sentence with a period, question mark, or exclamation point.
• Include details of what Amanda is like.

Finally, each lesson contains three blackline masters that teachers may photocopy to give students extra practice. Each of the three worksheets highlights a specific area—vocabulary, comprehension, and writing. Use the blackline masters to reteach, scaffold, or extend the lesson.

Name _____

Vocabulary

WORDS FROM THE SELECTION

Directions: Draw a line from each word to its meaning.

ballet   make your home in

house   12 o'clock at night

live   a kind of dancing

perfume   place to live in

midnight   sweet smell

WORD STUDY: Compound Words

A compound word is a word made up of two smaller words.

whenever = when + ever

Directions: Write the 2 small words in each compound word.

softball = soft + ball

grandma = _____

sandbox = _____

ladybug = _____

inside = _____

Name _____

Comprehension

CHECKING UNDERSTANDING

Directions: Read each sentence. Circle "T" if the sentence is **true** or "F" if the sentence is **false**.

T F 1. Amanda wants to move far away from her family.

T F 2. Amanda wants to do lots of things when she grows up.

T F 3. Amanda loves eggs.

T F 4. Amanda does not like perfume.

T F 5. Amanda likes to be with her mother.

RETELLING THE STORY

Directions: Write what Amanda wants on the lines below.

_____

_____

Name _____

Writing

CAPITAL LETTERS AND PERIODS

Directions: Mark an X in front of each sentence that starts with a capital letter and ends with a period.

_____1. Amanda wants to move far away from her family.

_____2. amanda wants to be a cook and a doctor.

_____3. amanda loves eggs.

_____4. Amanda is brave.

_____5. Amanda will be busy.

WRITING

Directions: Write a sentence that explains something you might like to do when you grow up.

_____

_____

_____

_____

_____

91

Daybooks *Research Base*

by April D. Nauman, Ph.D.

Introduction

Teachers today must find new, effective resources for helping students improve their literacy skills. The *Daybooks* provide this resource. Designed by educators, these journal-like paperbacks can help students become active, engaged, critical readers. The books provide students with the opportunity to regularly read and write responses to good literature. The books contain lessons in critical reading, literature selections, and spaces for students to write responses. The strategies and activities in the *Daybooks* are based in current research on how to improve student reading and writing ability.

One of the major goals of the *Daybooks* is to immerse students in quality literature. The passages selected for the books were recommended by panels of expert classroom teachers. At the high school level, the excerpts from contemporary authors are a valuable supplement to the standard curriculum. For the younger grades, the literature in the *Daybooks* may be used to enrich basal programs or as the core of a literature-based program. The difficulty levels of the selections are varied, which provides students with opportunities to read comfortably as well as to challenge themselves. These high-quality works also span a range of genres, from fiction to nonfiction.

Other major goals of the *Daybooks* are to promote students' ability to read actively; to build essential skills, such as questioning, summarizing, and finding the main idea, for reading well; to develop an appreciation for the elements of fiction, poetry, and nonfiction; and to foster an appreciation of language. These goals are accomplished through the introduction of strategies and activities drawn from the best available research in education today.

The Reading-Writing Connection

Educators and researchers have clearly established that reading and writing abilities develop together (e.g., Calkins, 1983; Pearson & Tierney, 1984; Shanahan, 1990; Sulzby & Teale, 1991; Tierney & Shanahan, 1991). Both processes are constructive and require similar kinds of knowledge. Teaching reading and writing together enhances communication, improves academic achievement, and leads to critical thinking (Cooper, 2000). Teachers who foster the construction of meaning through integrated reading and writing activities enable their students to become better thinkers (Tierney & Shanahan, 1991).

The *Daybooks* connect reading and writing in many important ways. Students are asked to read and respond creatively to literature excerpts. Also, students are prompted to jot down questions about the text, to brainstorm on the page, and to annotate the selections by underlining and highlighting. The varied writing activities in the *Daybooks* help students become better constructors of meaning.

The *Daybooks* encourage students to read and write frequently, even daily. Research has shown that students improve their literacy skills when they have the time and opportunity to practice these skills regularly. Most teachers agree that students "learn to read and write by reading and writing" (Cooper, 2000, p. 342), which underscores the need for frequent literacy opportunities. In addition, major writing educators emphasize the need for daily writing to enhance writing and reading ability (Atwell, 1998; Calkins, 1994; Graves, 1994). Recently, the U.S. Department of Education, in its summary of evidence-based reading instruction essential to the *No Child Left Behind* initiative, identified frequent writing opportunities as one of the important aspects of literacy instruction (U.S. Department of Education, 2001).

The writing activities included in the *Daybooks* are based in reader response research and theory. Reader response activities enhance both students' motivation to read and their ability to comprehend (Ruddell, 2002). Students given opportunities to respond to literature have been found to develop a sense of ownership over their learning (Hansen, 1987). Because constructing meaning relies on the reader's prior knowledge, each reader's meaning construction is individual and personal (Rosenblatt, 1978). Students given the opportunity to construct their own meanings learn to take responsibility for their own comprehension process. The opportunity to respond promotes students' monitoring of their own reading and writing (Cooper, 2000), which builds students' metacognitive processes (Palincsar & Brown, 1986; Paris, Wasik, & Turner, 1991). Instructional activities that promote comprehension monitoring are also endorsed by the National Reading Panel (2000), a panel of top U.S. educators recently convened to review the best available research in education today.

One excellent medium for responding to literature is journaling (Routman, 2000). Journaling allows for individual expression, engages all students in responses, and promotes active reading. Researchers have found that journaling in response to literature reinforces students' comprehension skills (Harste, Short, & Burke, 1988; Tierney, Readence, & Dishner, 1990). By journaling, students construct their own meanings and connect reading and writing (Atwell, 1998; Harste, et al., 1988; Parsons, 1990; Weaver, 1990). Responding to literature through journaling fosters introspection, deeper thinking, and metacognitive awareness (Routman, 2000). Such journaling "sensitizes" students to become more active in their reading, more deeply engaged with text (Atwell, 1998). Many types of journals have been described and are useful for promoting student response to literature (Cooper, 2000). The *Daybooks* are a unique type.

REFERENCES

Atwell, N. (1998). *In the middle: New understanding about writing, reading, and learning.* Portsmouth, NH: Boynton/Cook.

Calkins, L. M. (1983). *Lessons from a child on the teaching and learning of writing.* Exeter, NH: Heinemann.

Calkins, L. M. (1994). *The art of teaching writing.* Portsmouth, NH: Heinemann.

Cooper, J. D. (2000). *Literacy: Helping children construct meaning* (4th ed.). Boston: Houghton Mifflin.

Graves, D. H. (1994). *A fresh look at writing.* Portsmouth, NH: Heinemann.

Hansen, J. (1987). *When writers read.* Portsmouth, NH: Heinemann.

Harste, J. C., Short, K. G., and Burke, C. (1988). *Creating classrooms for authors.* Portsmouth, NH: Heinemann.

National Reading Panel (2000). *Teaching children to read: An evidence-based assessment of the scientific research literature on reading and its implications for reading instruction.* Washington, DC: National Institute of Child Health and Human Development.

Palincsar, A. S., & Brown, A. L. (1986). Interactive teaching to promote independent learning from text. *The Reading Teacher*, 39 (8), 771–777.

Paris, S. G., Wasik, B. A., & Turner, J. C. (1991). The development of strategic readers. In R. Barr, M. L. Kamil, P. B. Mosenthal, & P. D. Pearson (Eds.), *Handbook of reading research* (Vol. 2, pp. 609–640). New York: Longman.

Parsons, L. (1990). Response journals. Portsmouth, NH: Heinemann.

Pearson. P. D., & Tierney, R.J. (1984). On becoming a thoughtful reader: Learning to read like a writer. In A. C. Purves & O. Niles (Eds.), *Becoming readers in a complex society.* Eighty-third Yearbook of the National Society of the Study of Education (pp. 144–173). Chicago: University of Chicago Press.

Rosenblatt, L. M. (1978). *The reader, the text, the poem: The transactional theory of the literary work.* Carbondale, IL: Southern Illinois University Press.

Routman, R. (2000). *Conversations: Strategies for teaching, learning, and evaluating.* Portsmouth, NH: Heinemann.

Ruddell, R. B. (2002). *Teaching children to read and write: Becoming an effective literacy teacher* (3rd ed.). Boston: Allyn & Bacon.

Shanahan, T. (1990). Reading and writing together: What does it really mean? In T. Shanahan (Ed.), *Reading and writing together* (pp. 1–18). Norwood, MA: Christopher-Gordon.

Sulzby, E., & Teale, W. (1991). Emergent literacy. In R. Barr, M. L. Kamil, P. Mosenthal, & P. D. Pearson (Eds.), *Handbook of reading research* (Vol. 2, pp. 727–757), New York: Longman.

Tierney, R. J., Readence, J. E., & Dishner, E. K. (1990). Reading strategies and practices: A compendium (3rd ed.). Boston: Allyn & Bacon.

Tierney, R. J., & Shanahan, T. (1991). Research on the reading-writing relationship: Interactions, transactions, and outcomes. In R. Barr, M. L. Kamil, P. Mosenthal, & P. D. Pearson (Eds.), *Handbook of reading research* (Vol. 2, pp. 246–280), New York: Longman.

U.S. Department of Education Office of the Secretary (2001). *Back to school, moving forward: What No Child Left Behind means for America's communities.* Washington, DC.

Weaver, C. (1990). *Understanding whole language.* Portsmouth, NH: Heinemann.

Interacting with Text

One hallmark of successful reading is the ability to interact with or engage with text. Good readers are able to make connections with text in a variety of ways, whereas less capable readers are not (Wilhelm, 1997). Because comprehension relies on readers' ability to activate prior knowledge, connecting with text improves comprehension. To understand text, students must be able to link what they are reading to what they already know (Ruddell & Ruddell, 1994).

The *Daybooks* introduce and reinforce many skills that promote engagement with the text. Because the *Daybooks* belong to the students, they are free to mark up their texts, highlight and underline, jot down notes, or draw pictures in the margins as they progress through their reading. In each lesson, students are cued to respond at certain points in their reading and in specified places on the page. This level of support and practice helps all students gain a mastery of the active reading strategies they need to be successful readers.

In addition, the *Daybooks* introduce and reinforce strategies for active reading. For younger children, these strategies include predicting, questioning, and visualizing as well as marking up the text. For middle school children, the strategies include predicting, inferring, finding the main idea, identifying the author's purpose, and reflecting on reading. For high school students, the *Daybooks* reinforce strategies such as interacting with text and making personal connections as well as introduce important aspects of literary interpretation.

The value of these strategies has been demonstrated in a large body of research. Successful readers are known to approach reading strategically, using a variety of strategies to comprehend text (National Reading Panel, 2000; Pearson, Roehler, Dole, & Duffy, 1992; U.S. Department of Education, 2001). Predicting and questioning promote engagement with the text and improve comprehension (e.g., Harvey & Goudvis, 2000; Pearson, Roehler, Dole, & Duffy, 1992). Visualizing is also an important strategy, which struggling readers often lack (Harvey & Goudvis, 2000; Wilhelm, 1997). Summarizing during reading helps students build the habit of monitoring their comprehension (Cooper, 2000; Morrow, 2001; Tompkins, 1998). Finding the main idea, or distinguishing between important and unimportant information, is a related strategy that students need to learn to be successful readers (Alvermann & Moore, 1991; Cooper, 2000). The ability to make inferences while reading—to use prior knowledge to "fill in the gaps" in a text—is also essential to successful reading (van den Broek & Kremer, 2000). Instruction in the strategy of inference increases students' reading comprehension (Vacca & Vacca, 2002).

<u>REFERENCES</u>

Alvermann, D. E., & Moore, D. W. (1991). Secondary schools. In R. Barr, M. L. Kamil, P. B. Mosenthal, & P. D, Pearson (Eds.), *Handbook of reading research* (Vol. 2, pp. 951–983). New York: Longman.

Cooper, J. D. (2000). *Literacy: Helping children construct meaning* (4th ed.). Boston: Houghton Mifflin.

Harvey, S., & Goudvis, A. (2000). *Strategies that work: Teaching comprehension to enhance understanding*, Portland, ME: Stenhouse.

Morrow, L. M. (2001). *Literacy development in the early years: Helping children read and write* (4th ed.). Boston: Allyn & Bacon.

National Reading Panel (2000). *Teaching children to read: An evidence-based assessment of the scientific research literature on reading and its implications for reading instruction.* Washington, DC: National Institute of Child Health and Human Development.

Pearson, P. D., Roehler, L. R., Dole, J. A., & Duffy, G. G. (1992). Developing expertise in reading comprehension. In S. J. Samuels & A. E. Farstrup (Eds.), *What research has to say about reading instruction.* Newark, DE: International Reading Association.

Routman, R. (2000). *Conversations: Strategies for teaching, learning, and evaluating.* Portmsouth, NH: Heinemann.

Ruddell, R. B., & Ruddell, M. R. (1994). Language acquisition and literacy process. In R. B. Ruddell, M. R. Ruddell, & H. Singer (Eds.), *Theoretical models and processes of reading* (4th ed., pp. 448–468). Newark, DE: International Reading Association.

Tompkins, G. E. (1998). *50 literacy strategies: Step by step.* Upper Saddle River, NJ: Merrill Prentice Hall.

U.S. Department of Education Office of the Secretary (2001). *Back to school, moving forward: What No Child Left Behind means for America's communities.* Washington, DC.

Vacca, R. T., & Vacca, J. L. (2002). *Content area reading: Literacy and learning across the curriculum* (7th ed.). Boston: Allyn & Bacon.

van den Broek, P., & Kremer, K. E. (2000), The mind in action: What it means to comprehend during reading. In B. M. Taylor, M. F. Graves, & P. van den Broek (Eds.), *Reading for meaning: Fostering comprehension in the middle grades* (pp. 1–31). New York: Teachers College Press.

Wilhelm, J. (1997). *"You gotta BE the book": Teaching engaged and reflecting reading with adolescents.* New York: Teachers College Press.

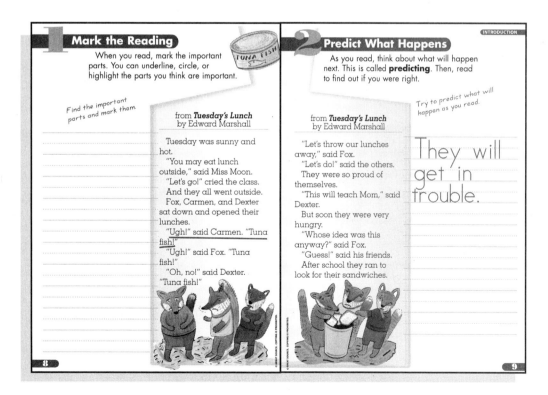

Reading Critically

The *Daybooks* foster students' ability to read critically through the Five Angles of Literacy. The Five Angles help students go beyond basic reading skills, building the ability to read critically and write effectively. The Angles of Literacy represent five approaches to effective critical literacy (Vinz, Reid, & Claggett, 1996). For each Angle, a set of strategies is taught and reinforced through practice.

For elementary school children, the Angles of Literacy involve learning and practicing strategies for active reading (such as highlighting and underlining, questioning, predicting, and visualizing); reading well (such as predicting, identifying the main idea, making inferences); reading fiction and nonfiction (understanding sequence and textual elements); understanding language (including similes and metaphors); and studying favorite authors. Students in the middle grades learn strategies for becoming active readers, making story connections, understanding the author's perspective, and focusing on language and craft.

At the high school level, the Angles of Literacy are explored in more depth. Students are encouraged to move gradually from the initial stage of engagement to more interpretive and evaluative approaches to text, in which they study authors' language, craft, lives, and work. Moving students from engagement to interpretation and finally to evaluation is supported by major reader response theorists (e.g., Rosenblatt, 1978).

The first Angle is interacting with a text, which promotes active, engaged reading. The strategies introduced to scaffold student ability to interact with text include underlining key phrases, writing questions or comments in the margins, noting word patterns and repetitions, circling unknown words, and keeping track of the story or idea as it unfolds. Rereading, summarizing, and generating questions, all important to successful comprehending (e.g., Heilman, Blair, & Rupley, 2002), are some of the activities in which students engage.

The second Angle is making connections to stories. Activities that promote such connection include making a story chart (e.g., Cooper, 2000; Freedle, 1979), connecting stories to events in one's own life (e.g., Routman, 2000; Ruddell & Ruddell, 1994), and speculating on the meaning or significance of story incidents. Connecting with stories enhances student engagement, motivation, and comprehension.

The third Angle of Literacy is shifting perspectives to examine a text from many viewpoints. Students learn to do this by examining point of view, changing the point of view, exploring various versions of an event, forming interpretations, comparing texts, and asking "what if" questions. When students learn to ask higher-level, "literary" questions, they begin to consider multiple possibilities and are motivated to look at the literature more carefully (Routman, 2000).

The fourth Angle is studying language and craft in a selection. This includes understanding figurative language, examining how the writer uses words, and studying a variety of types of literature. The ability to read "attentively and imaginatively," with an awareness of how authors use language, enhances the reader's enjoyment of a story (Charters, 1999). In addition, attention to the elements of quality literature has a positive impact on students' own writing (Calkins, 1994).

The fifth Angle of Literacy is studying the author, focusing on his or her life and work. Author study involves reading what the author says about his or her work, reading what others say about the work, making inferences about connections between the author's life and work, analyzing the author's style, and paying attention to repeating themes and topics in several works by one author. An awareness of the writer behind the work is essential to reading critically, enabling students to identify the author's purpose and point of view as well as distinguish fact from opinion (Roe, Stoodt, & Burns, 1998). The ability to "question the author" improves reading engagement and comprehension (Beck, McKeown, Hamilton, & Kucan, 1997).

The Angles of Literacy foster students' ability to read critically and write effectively. The strategies and activities provided in the *Daybooks* help students understand, practice, and gain control of the Angles of Literacy, enabling students to transfer their skills and become autonomous critical readers.

REFERENCES

Beck, I. L., McKeown, M. G., Hamilton, R., and Kucan, L. (1997). *Questioning the author: An approach for enhancing student engagement with text.* Newark, DE: International Reading Association.

Calkins, L. M. (1994). *The art of teaching writing.* Portsmouth, NH: Heinemann.

Charters, A. (1999). *The story and its writer.* (5th ed.). Boston: Bedford/St. Martin's.

Cooper, J. D. (2000). *Literacy: Helping children construct meaning* (4th ed.). Boston: Houghton Mifflin.

Freedle, R. P. (1979). *New directions in discourse processing.* Hillsdale, NJ: Lawrence Erlbaum.

Heilman, A. W., Blair, T. R., & Rupley, W. H. (2002). *Principles and practices of teaching reading* (10th ed.). Upper Saddle River, NJ: Merrill Prentice Hall.

Roe, B. D., Stoodt, B. D., and Burns, P. C. (1998). *The content areas* (6th ed.). Boston: Houghton Mifflin.

Rosenblatt, L. M. (1978). *The reader, the text, the poem: The transactional theory of the literary work.* Carbondale, IL: Southern Illinois University Press.

Routman, R. (2000). *Conversations: Strategies for teaching, learning, and evaluating.* Portsmouth, NH: Heinemann.

Ruddell, R. B., & Ruddell, M. R. (1994). Language acquisition and literacy process. In R. B. Ruddell, M. R. Ruddell, & H. Singer (Eds.), *Theoretical models and processes of reading* (4th ed., pp. 448–468). Newark, DE: International Reading Association.

Vinz, R., Reid, L., and Claggett, F. (1996). *Recasting the text.* Portsmouth, NH: Boynton.

Literacy Growth in the *Daybooks*

The *Daybooks* provide a valuable written record of student progress for assessment by teachers, parents, and the students themselves. Teachers may view the *Daybooks* as a type of portfolio—an ongoing, authentic measure of students' reading and writing ability. Portfolios are generally considered valuable tools for documenting, analyzing, and understanding students' reading and writing growth over time (e.g., Routman, 2000; Ruddell, 2002; Tompkins, 2001; Vacca & Vacca, 2002). In the *Daybooks*, students create a variety of responses that can be used for effective evaluation, such as summaries and reflections on readings (Cooper, 2000). Parents will also be interested to see the growth in their children's literacy skills.

In addition, this unique record of progress can also promote student self-assessment, which is an essential part of literacy evaluation (Flood & Lapp, 1989; Tierney, Carter, & Desai, 1991). Students can look back over their *Daybooks* to see how much they have learned and improved during a particular school year and may also compare their *Daybooks* from year to year. These records of progress can be used to enhance students' self-esteem and set a direction for future learning.

Because students literally own their *Daybooks,* students can experience a sense of ownership over their literacy progress. This sense of ownership is an important part of students' motivation to become readers and writers, their ability to persist in their literacy learning, and the development of a positive view of themselves as readers and writers. A sense of ownership also leads to a sense of responsibility for students' own learning. Combining ownership with opportunities for personal, creative involvement with quality literature, the *Daybooks* are a valuable addition to literacy curricula in elementary school, middle school, and high school.

REFERENCES

Cooper, J. D. (2000). *Literacy: Helping children construct meaning* (4th ed.). Boston: Houghton Mifflin.

Flood, J., & Lapp, D. (1989). Reporting reading progress: A comparison portfolio for parents. *Reading Teacher,* 42 (7), 508–514.

Routman, R. (2000). *Conversations: Strategies for teaching, learning, and evaluating.* Portsmouth, NH: Heinemann.

Ruddell, R. B. (2002). *Teaching children to read and write: Becoming an effective literacy teacher* (3rd ed.). Boston: Allyn & Bacon.

Tierney, R. J., Carter, M. A., & Desai, L. E. (1991). *Portfolio assessment in the reading-writing classroom.* Norwood, MA: Christopher-Gordon.

Tompkins, G. E. (2001). *Literacy for the 21st century* (2nd ed.). Upper Saddle River, NJ: Merrill Prentice Hall.

Vacca, R. T., & Vacca, J. L. (2002). *Content area reading: Literacy and learning across the curriculum* (7th ed.). Boston: Allyn & Bacon.

Introducing the Reading Process

Introduction

How do you teach your students about the writing process? You probably introduce students to the idea and model for them the steps in the process. You talk about the writing process in class, and then you walk through the steps with students on an actual assignment.

Just as writing is a process with several steps (prewriting, drafting, revising, editing and proofreading, and publishing), so, too, is reading. Start your students off right by explaining that reading is not an act (something you do and then are done with) but rather a process that takes place in a series of steps or stages. By doing so, you will help students begin to learn the series of actions—setting a purpose, previewing, planning, connecting with the text, and so on—that good readers automatically do.

The Process

Why should you teach your students about the reading or the writing process? The reason is that both reading and writing are complicated activities. They may seem easy to us, now that we are proficient at them. But remember that we all were novices at one time, struggling to put together everything a reader needs to know to pull meaning from a text.

A process breaks down a complicated activity into a series of smaller steps. Helping students to take one step at a time will be easier than trying to teach them to do everything at once. The reading process helps them remember the order of the steps, as well as what specifically to do Before, During, and After Reading, until finally those activities become automatic.

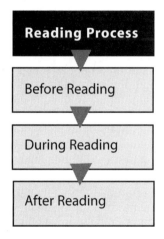

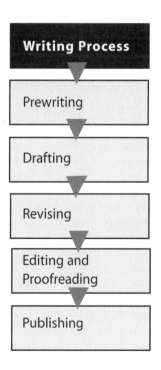

Before Reading

Before they read, proficient readers probably take at least three steps:

1. Set a purpose for reading.
2. Preview what they are going to read.
3. Plan how to read the selection.

Students are just learning the practices of good readers. As beginning readers, they will need help in taking these initial steps before reading. As the teacher, you can help students develop a sense of the reading process by using the *Teacher's Guide.*

Set a Purpose

Use the title of the lesson and objective at the beginning to help students understand their purpose for reading.

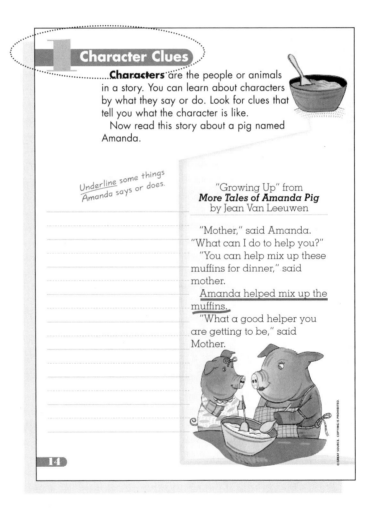

Preview

Two activities in the *Teacher's Guide* help students build background about each selection. The **Vocabulary** activity introduces students to words they will find in the selection. The **Prereading** activity helps students learn about the ideas and topic of the selection. You can also ask students to page through the entire selection and preview the pictures, which will build even more background for what they are about to read.

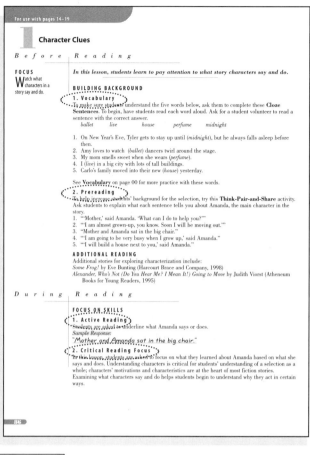

For use with pages 14–19

Character Clues

B e f o r e   R e a d i n g

FOCUS
Watch what characters in a story say and do.

In this lesson, students learn to pay attention to what story characters say and do.

BUILDING BACKGROUND

1. Vocabulary
To make sure students understand the five words below, ask them to complete these **Cloze Sentences**. To begin, have students read each word aloud. Ask for a student volunteer to read a sentence with the correct answer.

    ballet   live   house   perfume   midnight

1. On New Year's Eve, Tyler gets to stay up until (*midnight*), but he always falls asleep before then.
2. Amy loves to watch (*ballet*) dancers twirl around the stage.
3. My mom smells sweet when she wears (*perfume*).
4. I (*live*) in a big city with lots of tall buildings.
5. Carlo's family moved into their new (*house*) yesterday.

See **Vocabulary** on page 00 for more practice with these words.

2. Prereading
To help increase students' background for the selection, try this **Think-Pair-and-Share** activity. Ask students to explain what each sentence tells you about Amanda, the main character in the story.

1. "'Mother,' said Amanda. 'What can I do to help you?'"
2. "'I am almost grown-up, you know. Soon I will be moving out.'"
3. "Mother and Amanda sat in the big chair."
4. "'I am going to be very busy when I grow up,' said Amanda."
5. "'I will build a house next to you,' said Amanda."

ADDITIONAL READING
Additional stories for exploring characterization include:
Some Frog! by Eve Bunting (Harcourt Brace and Company, 1998)
Alexander, Who's Not (Do You Hear Me? I Mean It!) Going to Move by Judith Viorst (Atheneum Books for Young Readers, 1995)

D u r i n g   R e a d i n g

FOCUS ON SKILLS

1. Active Reading
Students are asked to underline what Amanda says or does.
Sample Response:
"Mother and Amanda sat in the big chair."

2. Critical Reading Focus
In this lesson, students are asked to focus on what they learned about Amanda based on what she says and does. Understanding characters is critical for students' understanding of a selection as a whole; characters' motivations and characteristics are at the heart of most fiction stories. Examining what characters say and do helps students begin to understand why they act in certain ways.

Character Clues

Characters are the people or animals in a story. You can learn about characters by what they say or do. Look for clues that tell you what the character is like.

Now read this story about a pig named Amanda.

Underline some things Amanda says or does.

"Growing Up" from
More Tales of Amanda Pig
by Jean Van Leeuwen

"Mother," said Amanda. "What can I do to help you?"

"You can help mix up these muffins for dinner," said mother.

<u>Amanda helped mix up the muffins.</u>

"What a good helper you are getting to be," said Mother.

14

Plan

The plan for how to read the selection is shown in red above the Response Notes. It tells students what to look for and how to mark up the text or take notes as they read. In the *Daybook*, students are always encouraged to read actively.

During Reading

As you read, you know what you are looking for, so you read with a purpose. You also probably connect what you are reading to what's going on in your life. Students, too, can read with a purpose and connect to what they read if you help guide them. The **Active Reading** example, the **Critical Reading Focus**, and the **highlighted text selections** in each lesson of the *Teacher's Guide* help you keep students focused on what they're reading. In the During Reading stage, have students:

1. Read with a purpose.
2. Connect what they read to what they know.

Read with a Purpose

The *Daybook* encourage students to read with a purpose by stating what to look for as they read. In all lessons, directions in red at the beginning of the lesson tell students what to look for. An example of what the direction means and what exactly students ought to do is shown in red.

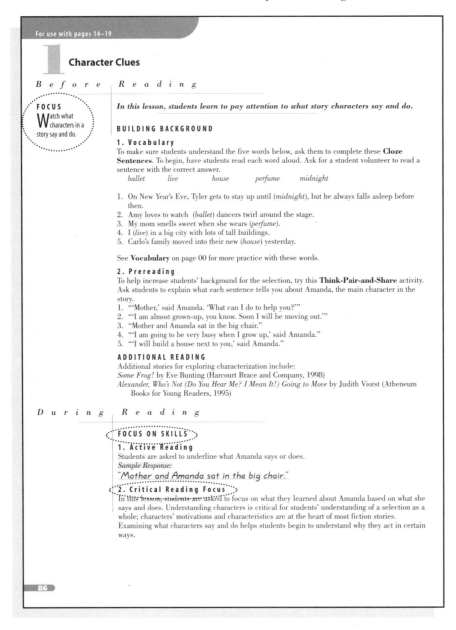

Connect

By helping students become active readers, the *Daybook* works to promote the connection between the text and the reader. Encourage students to relate what they read to their own lives and consider what they think as readers about the text. By promoting this engagement, you will build students' motivation to read, helping them see how a selection is relevant or important to them. Throughout the *Daybook*, you will see questions asking students what their opinions are. Honoring students' opinions and interests as readers will encourage them to connect with what they read.

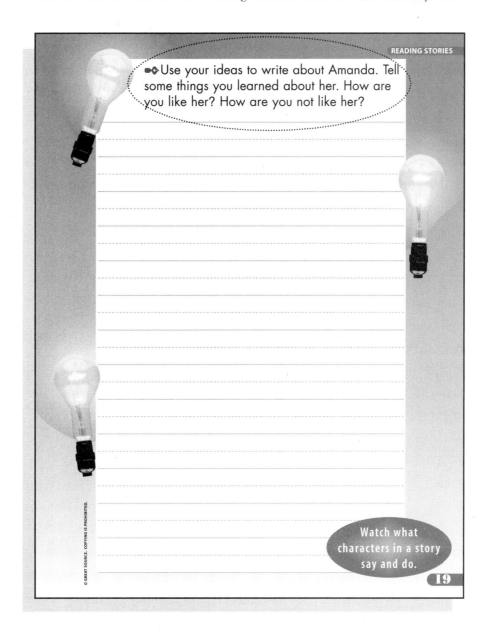

READING STORIES

➤Use your ideas to write about Amanda. Tell some things you learned about her. How are you like her? How are you not like her?

Watch what characters in a story say and do.

© GREAT SOURCE. COPYING IS PROHIBITED.

19

After Reading

After students read, they are usually glad just to be done and to have that work behind them. The *Daybook* encourages students to reflect on what they have read, because reflecting helps build comprehension. Encourage students to complete the entire reading process by taking three critical steps after they finish reading the last words in a selection:

1. Stop, reflect, and look back to see if they have met their reading purpose.
2. Go back and reread, as necessary, to find any information or details they might have missed.
3. Remember what they've read by writing or talking about the information or ideas they've learned.

Pause and Reflect

Immediately after finishing the last words in a selection, encourage students to stop a minute, look back, and think about what they have read. By modeling this behavior, you show students what good readers automatically do. You will also help students improve their comprehension. Did they meet their reading purpose? Good readers go back and "patch up" their understanding by rereading, and your students should too. The **Discussing the Literature** section in the *Teacher's Guide* provides sample questions to help students monitor their comprehension.

Reread

The activities in the *Daybook* are designed to challenge students enough that they have to go back into the text to complete them. Encourage your students to reread. Each lesson in the *Teacher's Guide* contains a specific rereading suggestion. Often students will be completely occupied with decoding words and extracting meaning from the syntax of sentences. To find a detail or main idea may require a second reading just for this purpose, once the general meaning of the text is clear. Be sure students understand that you think rereading is an important part of responding to the activities after the selections.

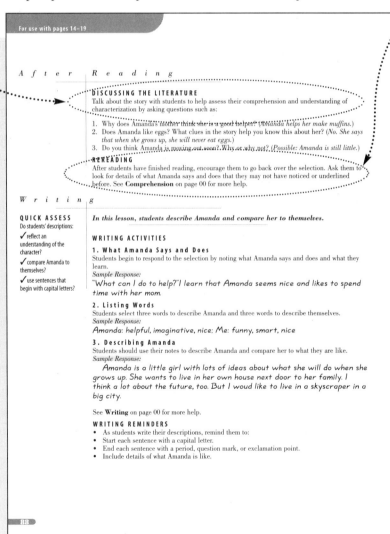

For use with pages 14–19

After Reading

DISCUSSING THE LITERATURE
Talk about the story with students to help assess their comprehension and understanding of characterization by asking questions such as:

1. Why does Amanda's Mother think she is a good helper? (*Amanda helps her make muffins.*)
2. Does Amanda like eggs? What clues in the story help you know this about her? (*No. She says that when she grows up, she will never eat eggs.*)
3. Do you think Amanda is growing out soon? Why or why not? (*Possible: Amanda is still little.*)

REREADING
After students have finished reading, encourage them to go back over the selection. Ask them to look for details of what Amanda says and does that they may not have noticed or underlined before. See **Comprehension** on page 00 for more help.

Writing

QUICK ASSESS
Do students' descriptions:
✓ reflect an understanding of the character?
✓ compare Amanda to themselves?
✓ use sentences that begin with capital letters?

In this lesson, students describe Amanda and compare her to themselves.

WRITING ACTIVITIES

1. What Amanda Says and Does
Students begin to respond to the selection by noting what Amanda says and does and what they learn.
Sample Response:
"What can I do to help?"/ I learn that Amanda seems nice and likes to spend time with her mom.

2. Listing Words
Students select three words to describe Amanda and three words to describe themselves.
Sample Response:
Amanda: helpful, imaginative, nice; Me: funny, smart, nice

3. Describing Amanda
Students should use their notes to describe Amanda and compare her to what they are like.
Sample Response:
Amanda is a little girl with lots of ideas about what she will do when she grows up. She wants to live in her own house next door to her family. I think a lot about the future, too. But I woud like to live in a skyscraper in a big city.

See **Writing** on page 00 for more help.

WRITING REMINDERS
- As students write their descriptions, remind them to:
- Start each sentence with a capital letter.
- End each sentence with a period, question mark, or exclamation point.
- Include details of what Amanda is like.

Remember

Readers remember things that mean something to them. By asking students to write about what they read or to complete a graphic organizer, the *Daybook* helps students make the reading their own. In doing so, the *Daybook* helps students remember the selection they have read. All lessons in the *Teacher's Guide* contain at least one writing activity to be completed in the **After Reading** stage.

What are 3 words that describe Amanda?

What are 3 words that describe you?

READING STORIES

Use your ideas to write about Amanda. Tell some things you learned about her. How are you like her? How are you not like her?

Watch what characters in a story say and do.

18

19

Summary

The *Daybook* encourages students to read and write and to use the reading process. Through its design, students will build the habits and acquire the practices of good readers and writers.

The *Daybook* attempts to develop better readers—ones that read actively by marking up the text, highlighting, questioning, predicting, and visualizing. The numerous, brief selections throughout the *Daybook* provide students with many opportunities to become more fluent, more active readers.

But the many different selections also can pose challenges for younger readers. With each selection, students meet new vocabulary, new subjects, new characters—in short, new challenges. To help students overcome these challenges, the Reading Workshop presented here offers students tools they can use to help them succeed.

Fifteen tools and corresponding mini-lessons for teachers are presented in the Workshop. Each mini-lesson includes a detailed explanation of what the tool is, how to use it, what it looks like, and what to look out for when using it with your class, followed by a do-it-yourself blackline master for you to adapt to individual *Daybook* lessons.

Table of Contents

Anticipation Guide

What Is It?

An Anticipation Guide serves two purposes: it helps motivate students to want to read a story or piece of nonfiction, and it builds background about the selection before students begin reading. As a result, it becomes a powerful tool in your arsenal for creating reading readiness in your students. To make an Anticipation Guide, write 3–5 statements about the subject of the selection.

How to Introduce It

Tell students that, before they read the next selection, you want to find out how much they already know about its subject. Then hand out copies of the Anticipation Guide that you create from the blackline master on the next page.

Have students write whether they agree or disagree with each statement. Then have students make a prediction about the story based on the statements from the Anticipation Guide.

What It Looks Like

An Anticipation Guide looks something like this:

Directions: Read each sentence. Circle whether you agree or disagree.
Return to the Anticipation Guide after reading.
See if your answers change.

Before Reading			After Reading	
1. Agree	Disagree	Elephants live by themselves.	Agree	Disagree
2. Agree	Disagree	Elephants are the largest animals.	Agree	Disagree
3. Agree	Disagree	Lions hunt for baby elephants.	Agree	Disagree
4. Agree	Disagree	Elephants are born with tusks.	Agree	Disagree

Now make a prediction. What do you think this selection will be about?

What to Look Out For

The idea behind an Anticipation Guide is to build background for students and provide motivation for what they are about to read. Along with making predictions about what they will read, have students form questions about their reading. Be sure to return to the Anticipation Guide after reading to give students a chance to modify their choices based on what they learned from the selection.

Name _____

Anticipation Guide

Selection: _____

Author: _____

Directions: Read each sentence. Circle whether you agree or disagree.

AGREE   DISAGREE   1. _____

_____

AGREE   DISAGREE   2. _____

_____

AGREE   DISAGREE   3. _____

_____

AGREE   DISAGREE   4. _____

_____

What do you think this selection will be about?

_____

_____

_____

C h a r a c t e r   M a p

What Is It?

A Character Map gives you a detailed picture of a single character from a story or novel. With this tool, students can look at a character from several points of view.

How to Introduce It

Explain that a Character Map is a tool to help students better understand the characters they read about. Filling in the Character Map helps them look at their characters in ways they might not have thought of before. Reluctant readers might work best in small groups or buddied up with a partner.

What it Looks Like

A Character Map looks something like this:

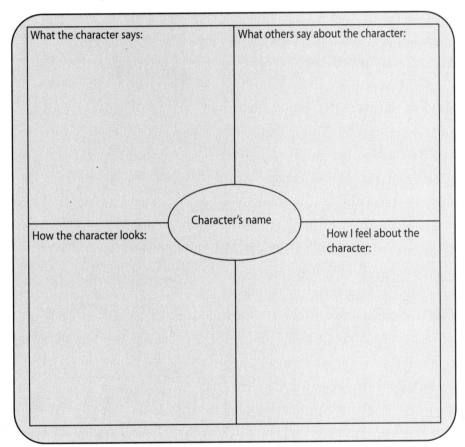

What to Look Out For

Some students may have trouble determining how they feel about the character beyond writing things like "ok" or "all right." Encourage students to dig deeper to look for more specific words to describe how they feel about the character.

Name

Character Map

Selection:

Author:

What the character says:	What others say about the character:

Character's name

How the character looks:

How I feel about the character:

C o n c e p t   W e b

What Is It?

A Concept Web is an excellent all-purpose tool that helps readers organize ideas before and after reading both fiction and nonfiction. Before reading, a Web can help students activate their prior knowledge. After reading, students can use a Web to help them brainstorm and categorize what they learned from their reading.

How to Introduce It

Hand out copies of the Concept Web on the next page. Have students write the name of the animal, thing, or concept in the middle circle. Then brainstorm with students some key questions about it to write on the lines, such as:
- What does it look like?
- What are some examples of it?
- What do you feel about it?
- How does it feel?
- What else do you know about it?

(These questions will change depending on the topic you are working with.)

What It Looks Like

A Concept Web looks something like this:

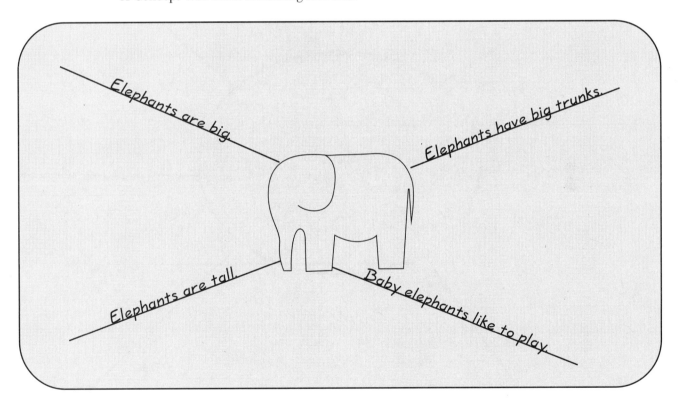

What to Look Out For

Remember that as a Before Reading tool, the goal of a Concept Web is to build background and activate prior knowledge on a subject. As an After Reading activity, the goal should be to organize and begin processing what students just read.

Concept Web

Selection:

Author:

Directions: Write the name of the subject of the Web in the center picture. Then answer the questions around it.

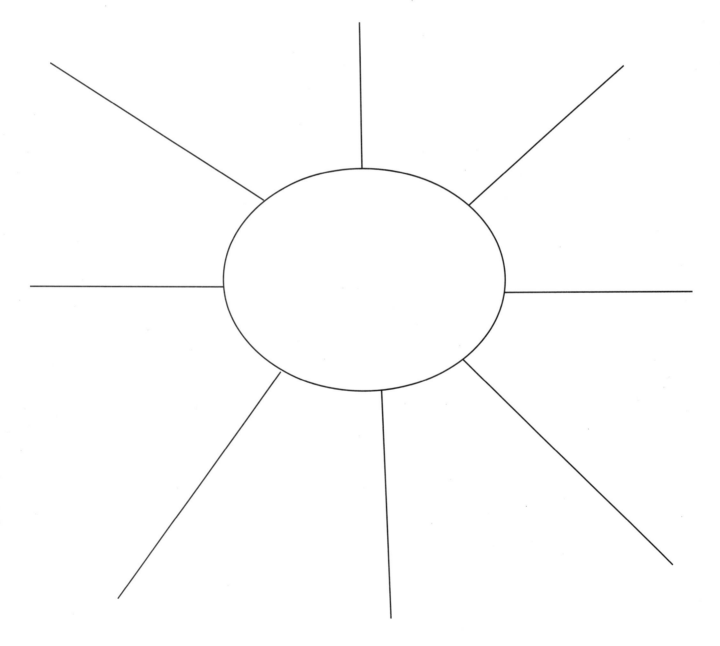

D o u b l e - e n t r y   J o u r n a l

What Is It?

A Double-entry Journal is a way to help students look closely at what they are reading. You write a quote or sentence from the selection in the left-hand column, and students respond by writing their reactions to the passage in the right-hand column. Double-entry Journals build students' ability to comprehend and interpret what they read.

How to Introduce It

Tell students that you will show them a way to help them better understand what they read. Create a Double-entry Journal on the board. Write a quote from a story the class is currently reading in the left-hand column. Perform a Think Aloud as you note your reactions to the quote to help students see how to respond in the second column. Invite student volunteers to share their responses to the quote as well. Make clear that there is no one "right" answer.

What It Looks Like

Here is an example of what a Double-entry Journal looks like. (At this early grade level, headings will change depending on the Journal's focus.)

Directions: Read each quote or sentence from the story in the first column.
Tell what you think about each quote in the second column.

Quotes from the Story	What I Think About Them
"And sometimes I have to settle disagreements between my co-workers."	Jamal is a good friend.
"Then I shoot a few hoops."	Jamal likes to play basketball.
"I set the table."	Jamal helps out at home.
"'I've had a busy day myself.'"	Jamal thinks his day at school is just as busy as his parents' day at work.
"But I can't wait until tomorrow."	Jamal likes going to school and keeping busy.

What to Look Out For

Students often get caught up trying to figure out the correct answer. Keep reinforcing the idea that a Double-entry Journal is not about right or wrong answers, but rather about how students feel about the passages pulled from the story. The more students can move beyond trying to get the correct answer, the more they will be able to respond authentically.

Double-entry Journal

Selection: _____

Author: _____

Directions: Read each quote or sentence from the story in the first column. Tell what you think about each quote in the second column.

Quotes from the Story	What I Think about Them

Main Idea and Details Organizer

What Is It?

A Main Idea and Details Organizer is a wonderful tool for understanding and remembering important information in nonfiction reading materials. Identifying the main idea is critical to understanding any piece of nonfiction. Providing consistent practice in identifying the main idea and supporting details from the earliest grades, including the use of tools such as this organizer, will help students develop one of the most essential reading skills.

How to Introduce It

Tell students that creating a Main Idea and Details Organizer when reading nonfiction can help them figure out what is the most important, or main, idea in a selection. Point out that knowing the main idea helps readers understand what the author is trying to tell them. Once students understand the main idea, they can separate details that support the main idea from less important information presented in the selection.

What It Looks Like

Here is an example of a Main Idea and Details Organizer:

Main Idea
The sun always shines.

Detail	Detail	Detail
The earth is always turning.	We turn away from the sun at night.	We turn back to the sun in the morning.

What to Look Out For

Finding the main idea can be tricky for students at first. Help them gain confidence in their ability to master this essential reading skill by thinking aloud as you identify the main idea in short passages or paragraphs. Help students see that the main idea is the most important idea that the author wants to tell the reader.

Main Idea and Details Organizer

Selection:

Author:

Directions: Tell about the main idea (the most important idea) in the Main Idea box. List 3 details about the main idea in the bottom Detail boxes.

Main Idea

Detail

Detail

Detail

P r e d i c t i n g   G u i d e

What Is It?

Often, we ask students to make predictions about a story's or selection's outcome. We forget to have students go back to those original predictions and check them to see how well they matched what actually happened. The *Daybook* contains many opportunities for students to make predictions. The Predicting Guide is a useful tool for helping both students and teachers remember the importance of going back and reflecting on those original predictions.

How to Introduce It

Tell students that they will be asked to make lots of predictions as they work through the *Daybook*. Make clear that there is never a right or wrong prediction—predictions are really guesses based on what you already know about a subject and what you think is going to happen. Pass out the Predicting Guide on the next page. Explain that this guide will help students keep track of their predictions when they read a story and also help them remember to go back to their predictions to see if they match what really happens in the story.

What It Looks Like

A Predicting Guide looks something like this:

Directions:	Use this paper to tell your predictions. Write your predictions about the story in the first column. After reading the story, write what really happened in the second column.

I Predict	What Really Happens
I predict this story is about a boy and his dog.	It is a story about a boy and his dog.

What to Look Out For

The biggest stumbling block with predictions is that students fear that there is a right answer, especially when you have them compare their predictions to what really happens in the story. Make clear that the reason for comparing predictions to what really happens is not to see whether students were "right" or "wrong" but rather to see how well they were able to pick up clues. Point out that how well students can make predictions about a certain subject depends on how much they know about that subject. If they know a lot about trains, they will probably be able to make better predictions about a book on trains than a book on stuffed animals. The more you can get students to relax about right and wrong answers, the more authentic their predictions will be.

Predicting Guide

Selection:

Author:

Directions: Write your predictions about the story in the first column. After reading the story, write what really happened in the second column.

I Predict	What Really Happens
I predict	
I predict	
I predict	

Previewing Checklist

What Is It?

Previewing is one of the most powerful Before Reading strategies for activating students' prior knowledge and providing motivation for reading a new selection. A Previewing Checklist can serve as an excellent tool for helping students keep their preview on target and to use the information they gain from their preview to make predictions about the reading,

How to Introduce It

Tell students that before they read the next story, they will preview it. Talk about what students know about previewing. Lead students to see that previewing a story helps them get a sense of what the story is all about before reading it so they can have a basic understanding of the text. Hand out the Previewing Checklist from the next page. Explain that the Checklist will help students as they preview the story and make a prediction about it.

What It Looks Like

A completed Previewing Checklist looks something like this:

Directions: Put a checkmark after you finish each activity.
Then tell what you learned from completing it.

_____X_____ Read title.
What clues does it give me about the story?

Too Many Tamales sounds likes someone ate too much and got

a tummy ache.

_____X_____ Look at the pictures.
What clues do they give me about the story?

It is Christmas. Someone makes tamales. There are lots of presents.

_____X_____ Read the first paragraph.
What clues does it give me about the story?

The story takes place at Christmas.

What to Look Out For

Remind students that previewing, like predicting, does not involve right or wrong answers. One student might see one idea in a picture, while another sees something else. Keep reinforcing that this is fine; the idea behind previewing is to get students thinking about the story and their prior knowledge about the subject of the story, not about whose ideas are more accurate.

Previewing Checklist

Selection:

Author:

Directions: Put a checkmark after you finish each activity. Then tell what you learned from completing it.

_____ Read title.

What clues does it give me about the story?

_____

_____

_____

_____

_____ Look at the pictures.

What clues do they give me about the story?

_____

_____

_____

_____

_____ What did I learn about the story from my preview?

What clues does it give me about the story?

_____

_____

_____

_____

P r o b l e m - S o l u t i o n   M a p

What Is It?

Problem-Solution Maps are most often associated with nonfiction in upper grades, but at lower grade levels they can be excellent tools for helping students recognize the central conflict of a story and how it is resolved.

How to Introduce It

Explain to students that all stories revolve around one or more problems. Have students brainstorm the problems and solutions associated with familiar fairy tales, such as The *Three Little Pigs* and *Goldilocks*. Help students see that without a problem to solve, stories would not be as fun to read. Point out that a Problem-Solution Map can help students find the story's problem and how it is solved.

What It Looks Like

A Problem-Solution Map looks something like this:

> **PROBLEM**
> *Every time the mouse throws a penny in the wishing well to make a wish, the wishing well says, "OUCH."*
>
> ↓
>
> **SOLUTION**
> *The mouse throws a pillow down the well so that when she drops the penny in it, it doesn't hurt the well any more. Now her wishes can come true.*

What to Look Out For

Often, stories have more than one problem. Help students identify the central problem by asking them to list all the problems they can find in the story and then circle the one problem that is most important for the characters to solve. Have students use that problem as the basis for their Problem-Solution Map.

Name _____

Problem-Solution Map

Selection: _____

Author: _____

Directions: Tell about the story's problem in the first box. Tell how the problem is solved in the second box.

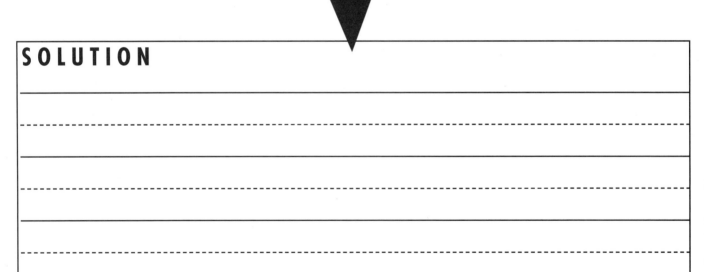

PROBLEM

_____

_____

_____

SOLUTION

_____

_____

_____

R e t e l l i n g   O r g a n i z e r

What Is It?

A retelling is a "telling again" of the story in the student's own words. Retelling gives students a chance to put the key events of the selection in their own words.

The act of processing what they comprehend and translating it into their own words helps students better understand and remember what they read.

How to Introduce It

Tell students that retelling a story in their own words will help them better understand and remember what they read. Explain that using a Retelling Organizer will help students determine what parts of the story should be included in their retelling.

What It Looks Like

Here is an example of a Retelling Organizer:

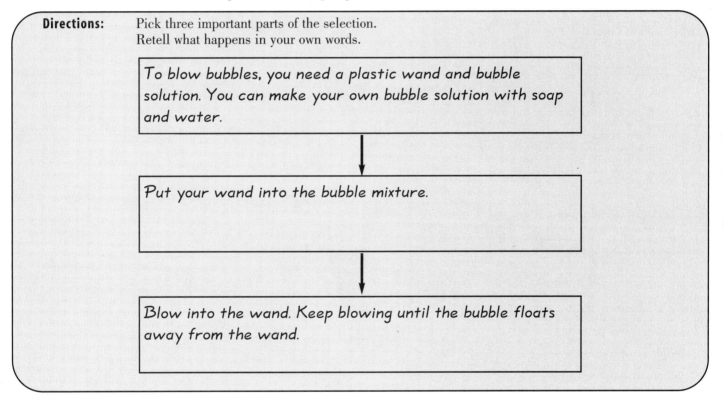

Directions: Pick three important parts of the selection.
Retell what happens in your own words.

> To blow bubbles, you need a plastic wand and bubble solution. You can make your own bubble solution with soap and water.

> Put your wand into the bubble mixture.

> Blow into the wand. Keep blowing until the bubble floats away from the wand.

What to Look Out For

Some students might have trouble retelling selections in their own words. To help them get started, invite them to first talk about the story with a partner. Ask students to imagine that their partners have never heard of the story. What would students tell them about the story? Have students use this oral retelling as a basis for their written retellings.

Retelling Organizer

Selection:

Author:

Directions: Pick four important parts of the selection. Retell what happens in your own words.

S e q u e n c e   C h a r t

What is it?

A Sequence Chart is an excellent introduction to keeping track of time-order relationships. While timelines are too sophisticated for this level, a more basic Sequence Chart can help students begin to see how authors use clue words such as *then* and *next* to indicate the passage of time.

How to Introduce It

Write out a list of sequence words on the board, such as *first, second, next, then,* and *finally*. Explain that these are words that authors use to tell their readers that time is passing in the story. These words also help the readers keep track of when certain events take place. Explain that a Sequence Chart is a great tool for keeping track of these events as well. Point out that a Sequence Chart can be used with both stories and nonfiction writing.

What It Looks Like

A Sequence Chart looks something like this once it is completed:

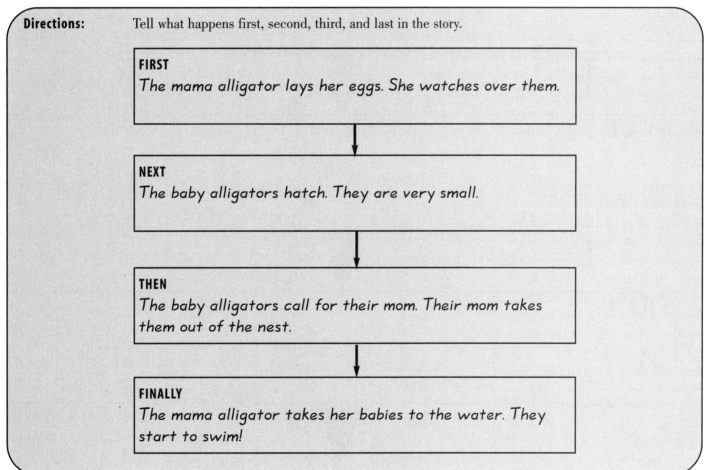

Directions: Tell what happens first, second, third, and last in the story.

FIRST
The mama alligator lays her eggs. She watches over them.

↓

NEXT
The baby alligators hatch. They are very small.

↓

THEN
The baby alligators call for their mom. Their mom takes them out of the nest.

↓

FINALLY
The mama alligator takes her babies to the water. They start to swim!

What to Look Out For

As with other organizers that involve retelling parts of the story, students can have trouble both deciding which parts of the story to include in the organizer and how to retell them in their own words. Encourage them to think back over the story to find the most important events—those that involve the story's problem and how it is solved—to include in the Sequence Chart.

Name

Sequence Chart

Selection: _____

Author: _____

Directions: Write what happens first, second, third, and last.

FIRST

▼

NEXT

▼

THEN

▼

FINALLY

S e t t i n g   C h a r t

What Is It?

A Setting Chart is a useful tool for helping readers keep track of when and where a story takes place. In some stories, the setting is not particularly important. But in other stories, such as *The Wizard of Oz* or *Willie Wonka and the Chocolate Factory*, understanding the setting is crucial to understanding the story as a whole. A Setting Chart can make the task much simpler.

How to Introduce It

Talk to students about a story's setting. Explain that using a Setting Chart will help them keep track of where and when a story takes place. Talk about the differences between *when* and *where*. Make clear that *when* tells about time while *where* tells about place.

What It Looks Like

Here is an example of a Setting Chart:

Directions: Write the name of the story and its author in the top box.
Tell about when the story takes place in the left-hand box.
Tell about where the story takes place in the right-hand box.

TITLE: *Henry and Mudge Under the Yellow Moon*	
AUTHOR: *Cynthia Rylant*	
When (Clues about Time):	**Where (Clues about Place):**
fall	*woods*
birds flying south	*falling leaves*

What to Look Out For

Most students find it relatively simple to find clues about setting in a story. What they might find challenging, however, is distinguishing between clues about time and clues about place. To help them, encourage students to ask themselves, "Does this clue about the setting tell me about *when* the story takes place or *where* the story takes place?"

Name

Setting Chart

Selection:

Author:

Directions: Write the name of the story and its author in the top box. Tell about when the story takes place in the left-hand box. Tell about where the story takes place in the right-hand box.

TITLE: AUTHOR:	
WHEN (Clues about Time):	WHERE (Clues about Place):

Use your Setting Chart to describe the setting of the story.

Story String

What Is It?

A Story String is an excellent tool for summarizing key plot events in a story. Whereas more traditional plot organizers require students to identify the climax, resolution, and so on, all that is required in a Story String is for students to retell the events in correct order. Therefore, it is a more appropriate organizer for younger students.

How to Introduce It

Explain to students that using a reading tool such as a Story String can help them retell and remember important events in a story. Talk with students about how to choose the events to include in a Story String. Help students see that they cannot include everything that happens in a story. Instead, they have to decide which events are most important. Point out to students that one way to figure out what's important is to first figure out what the main problem in the story is and then include events that involve the problem.

What It Looks Like

A Story String looks something like this:

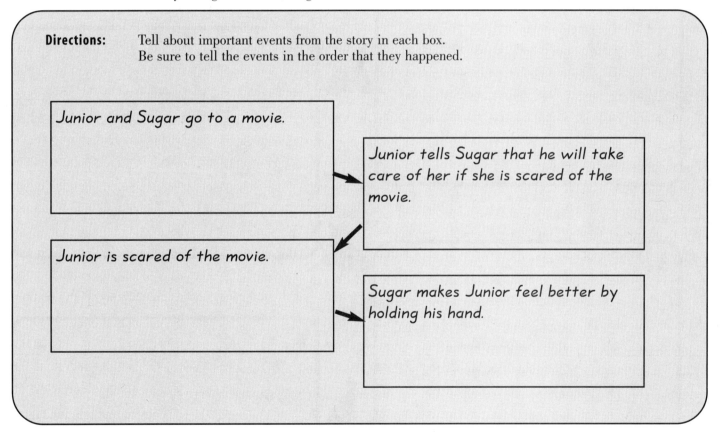

Directions: Tell about important events from the story in each box.
Be sure to tell the events in the order that they happened.

Junior and Sugar go to a movie.

Junior tells Sugar that he will take care of her if she is scared of the movie.

Junior is scared of the movie.

Sugar makes Junior feel better by holding his hand.

What to Look Out For

Remind students that they need to use their own words when they retell the events in the Story String. For those students who have trouble doing so, have them first imagine they are telling a friend about the story. What would they say? Encourage students to use their "talk" as the basis for their Story String.

Story String

Selection: _____

Author: _____

Directions: Write the most important events from the story in the boxes below. Be sure to tell the events in the order that they happened.

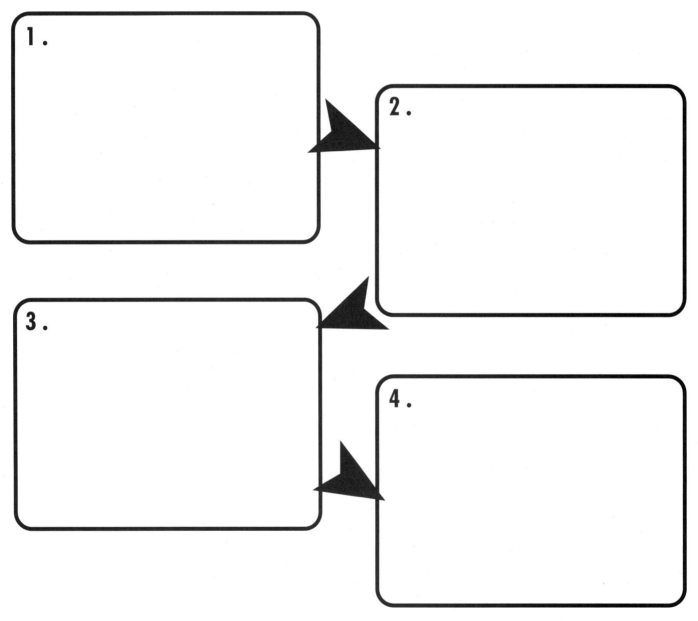

1.

2.

3.

4.

S t o r y b o a r d

What Is It?

A Storyboard gives students a chance to retell key parts of a story using another medium besides writing—artwork. Students pick three or four important parts of the story and sketch them. Then they write a brief description of the sketch. Storyboards are wonderful tools for students who have difficulty getting their thoughts down on paper or those whose creativity comes through best via drawing.

How to Introduce It

Tell students that there are many ways to retell a story and not all of the ways have to be done in writing. Hand out copies of the Storyboard blackline master from the next page. Explain to students that a Storyboard is a way to tell about important parts in a story by drawing them.

What It Looks Like

A completed Storyboard looks something like this:

Directions:	Draw two important events from the story. Describe each sketch.

Sketch	Description
	An owl is in the tree.
	The people watch the owl fly off.

What to Look Out For

Some students, particularly those who don't consider themselves very artistic, can be quite intimidated at first by the thought of having to create sketches. Keep reassuring them that the point of this activity is not to create masterpieces of art, but to show important events from the story, no matter how simple the sketches might be.

Name

Storyboard

Directions: Draw three important events from the story.
Describe each sketch.

Sketch	Description

Think-Pair-and-Share

What Is It?

A Think-Pair-and-Share activity introduces students to a selection in a fun, interactive way, gently leading even the most reluctant reader into the act of reading. It provides students with some background about a selection and piques interest in what will happen next.

How to Introduce It

Have students first work together in small groups of 4–6. If possible, write each sentence on a strip of paper. Give each student in the group one sentence and ask him or her to read it aloud. Tell students their job is to decide in what order the sentence appears in the selection. Come together as a class and compare the groups' ideas. As a whole class, talk about what students think the selection will be about or what they learned about a character.

What It Looks Like

Here is an example of a Think-Pair-and-Share activity:

Directions: First, put these sentences in the order you think they happen in the story.
Then, tell what you have learned about Amanda, the main character in the story.

_____ "Mother," said Amanda. "What can I do to help you?"

_____ "I am almost grown-up, you know. Soon I will be moving out."

_____ "I will be a ballet dancer," said Amanda.

_____ "I am going to be very busy when I grow up," said Amanda.

_____ "I will build a house next to you," said Amanda.

What have you learned about Amanda?

_____

_____

_____

What to Look Out For

Remind students that the purpose of this activity is not so much to get the "right" answer as to get them thinking about what the story will be about and to get them interested in reading it.

Think-Pair-and-Share

Selection:

Author:

Directions: First, number these sentences in the order you think they happen in the story. Then tell what you think about the story.

What do you think the story is about?

V o c a b u l a r y   I n v e n t o r y

What Is It?

A Vocabulary Inventory provides you with an understanding of how familiar students are with a selection's vocabulary. Quick and easy, the Inventory can be a great way to begin a lesson with challenging words, as well as a way to start students thinking about the selection, because the words can suggest the subject and be the starting point for making predictions about the selection.

How to Introduce It

Explain to students that you want to find out how well they know some of the words in the story. Point out that the purpose of a Vocabulary Inventory is to start thinking about some of the words from the story and what the story may be about.

What It Looks Like

A Vocabulary Inventory looks something like this:

Directions: Read each word. Then mark whether you know the word (+), seen it before but can't remember what it means (?), or do not know the word (0).

+ I Know This Word.
? I've Seen This Word Before But Can't Remember What It Means.
0 I Don't Know This Word.

1. __?__ plastic

2. __+__ float

3. __0__ shimmers

4. __+__ liquid

5. __0__ snaps

Now make a prediction. What do you think this selection will be about?

_____

_____

What to Look Out For

A Vocabulary Inventory will give you an idea of how well students can handle the vocabulary in the selection. If you find that students have difficulty with the words from the Inventory, take time before reading to provide definitions.

Vocabulary Inventory

Selection: _____

Author: _____

Directions: Read each word. Then mark whether you know the word (+), seen it but can't remember what it means (?), or do not know the word (0).

+ I Know This Word.

? I've Seen This Word But Can't Remember What It Means.

0 I Don't Know This Word.

1. ____ _____

2. ____ _____

3. ____ _____

4. ____ _____

5. ____ _____

Now make a prediction. What do you think this selection will be about?

_____

_____

_____

_____

LESSON
RESOURCES

Unit Overview

In this unit, students learn how to mark up a text, underline, highlight, predict, question, and visualize. The purpose of these initial lessons is to start students marking in the *Daybook* and writing in the Response Notes. The active reading skills introduced in these first lessons will be practiced throughout the *Daybook*, so students do not need mastery of active reading before progressing out of this unit. The idea of the introductory unit is to start students on the road toward becoming active readers.

Reading the Art

Be sure students take a moment to "read" the artwork. Have them study the image as they answer these questions:

- What do you see?
- How would you describe the look on the girl's face?
- How does the art make you feel?

Literature Focus

Lesson	Literature
1. Mark the Reading	**Edward Marshall,** from *Tuesday's Lunch*
	This selection is about three young foxes who dislike the food they have in their lunches.
2. Predict What Happens	**Edward Marshall,** from *Tuesday's Lunch*
	In this second part of the story, the three friends throw away their lunches, only to find themselves hungry in the afternoon.
3. Ask Questions	**Edward Marshall,** from *Tuesday's Lunch*
	In this conclusion, the three friends realize that an old cat has found their sandwiches and eaten them.
4. Draw What You See	**Edward Marshall,** from *Tuesday's Lunch*
	Students have an opportunity to draw a scene from the story.

Reading Focus

Lesson	Reading Skill
1. Mark the Reading	Mark, underline, and highlight parts of a text.
2. Predict What Happens	Use what you know and clues from a story to figure out what will happen next.
3. Ask Questions	Ask questions about the plot, setting, and characters as you read.
4. Draw What You See	Draw or sketch the pictures you see in your mind as you read.

Introduction: Active Reading

Before Reading

FOCUS

As you read, mark, ask questions, predict, and draw what you see.

In this lesson, students learn how marking up the text, asking questions, predicting, and visualizing can help them become more active readers.

BUILDING BACKGROUND

1. Vocabulary

cried   tuna   proud   idea   gosh

Before reading the selection, make sure students understand the above vocabulary words. Use a **Context Clues** activity to help them. Work with students to figure out the meaning of the underlined word in each sentence.

1. "'Let's go!' <u>cried</u> the class."
2. "'Ugh!' said Fox. '<u>Tuna</u> fish!'"
3. "They were so <u>proud</u> of themselves."
4. "'Whose <u>idea</u> was this anyway?' said Fox."
5. "'<u>Gosh</u>,' said the old cat. 'Kids are really smart these days.'"

See **Vocabulary** on page 81 for more practice with these words.

2. Prereading

Provide additional introduction to the selection by **Previewing** it as a whole class. Read the title and first three paragraphs aloud. Have students look at the illustrations. Then talk about the preview by discussing questions such as:

1. What is the selection about? (*It is about three foxes who do not like their lunches.*)
2. What does the title tell you about the story? (*It takes place on Tuesday, and it is about lunch.*)
3. What questions do you have about the story from previewing it? (*Possible: Why is the cat smiling?*)

ADDITIONAL READING

Additional stories by Edward Marshall include:
Fox All Week (Dial Books for Young Readers, 1984)
Fox and His Friends (Dial Press, 1982)
Space Case (Dial Press, 1980)

During Reading

FOCUS ON SKILLS

1. Active Reading

Students focus on different ways of reading actively. On page 8, they are asked to mark the important parts.

Sample Response:

"'Oh, no!' said Dexter. 'Tuna fish!'"

On page 9, they predict what will happen next.

Sample Response:

They will find their sandwiches.

On page 10, they ask questions as they read.

Sample Response:

Why is the cat so happy?

The pictures they draw on page 11 will vary.

2. Critical Reading Focus

One of the foremost goals of the *Daybooks* is to help students become more active readers. The four techniques discussed in this lesson will foster students' ability to read actively, find and remember important information, and stay focused on and involved with the reading.

D u r i n g   R e a d i n g

FOCUS ON THE SELECTION

Focus on key passages in the story to help students understand how to become more active readers.

from *Tuesday's Lunch*
by Edward Marshall

Page 8

Point out that all three friends share the same feelings about their lunches. Ask students, "Why is what Carmen, Fox, and Dexter say about their lunches important? What do you learn about the characters here?"

"Ugh!" said Carmen. "Tuna fish!"
"Ugh!" said Fox. "Tuna fish!"
"Oh no!" said Dexter. "Tuna fish!"

Page 9

Ask students, "What do you think will happen next? Why?"

After school they ran to look for their sandwiches.

Page 10

Ask students, "How does Fox probably feel now?"

"Three tuna sandwiches?" said Fox.
"Gosh," said the old cat. "Kids are really smart these days."

As you walk students through these parts of the reading, remind them to focus on important details in the story to back up their opinions and predictions. For example, students are likely to say that Fox feels unhappy and disappointed when he realizes the old cat ate the sandwiches. Encourage them to remember how proud the three friends had been at first when they threw out the lunches. Discuss together how they soon realized they had made a mistake. The old cat may think they are smart, but Fox and his friends may be feeling as if they did something stupid.

After Reading

DISCUSSING THE LITERATURE

Talk about the selection with students to help assess their comprehension of the story and understanding of active reading by asking questions such as:

1. What helped you the most as you read this story: marking important parts, predicting what would happen next, asking questions, or drawing a picture? Why? (*Possible: Making predictions helped me the most because I wanted to keep reading to see if my predictions came true.*)
2. Why does the cat think kids these days are smart? (*He is impressed that Fox knew what the lunch was.*)
3. Why is it important to be an active reader? (*Possible: Active readers understand what they read better.*)

REREADING

Encourage students to read the story again. Ask them what they noticed on this second reading that they might have missed before.

See **Comprehension** on page 82 for more help.

Writing

QUICK ASSESS
Do students' drawings:

✔ demonstrate an understanding of what is happening in the story?

✔ show creativity without adding elements not found in the story?

In this lesson, students mark important parts, make predictions, ask questions, and draw a picture of what happens in the story.

WRITING ACTIVITIES

1. Drawing What You See
Students respond to the selection by drawing a picture of what happened in the story.
Sample Response:

2. Reviewing
Students continue responding to the selection by reviewing the four active reading techniques. You may want to have them use a separate piece of paper and give an example of each technique they used as they read *Tuesday's Lunch.*

See **Writing** on page 83 for more help.

WRITING REMINDERS
As students draw their pictures, remind them to:
•   Include details from the story.
•   Be creative but do not include anything that is not part of the story.
•   Choose part of the story they can easily imagine.

Vocabulary

WORDS FROM THE SELECTION

Directions: Use words from the box to fill in each sentence.

| cried   tuna   idea   gosh |

1. The girl _____, "Oh _____,

   I wish I could get a kitten."

2. My sister likes _____, but I do not.

3. Fox had a great _____.

WORD STUDY: Contractions

Use an apostrophe to form a contraction. The apostrophe takes the place of one or more letters.

it is = it's   I will = I'll   do not = don't

Directions: Use the words in ( ) to make a contraction.

1. (They are) _____ funny characters.

2. Fox and his friends (did not) _____ eat lunch.

3. (I am) _____ surprised by the story's ending.

Comprehension

CHECKING UNDERSTANDING

Directions: Label the 4 kinds of active reading.

Write an M where the reader marked the story.

Write a P where the reader predicted.

Write a Q where the reader asked a question.

Write a D where the reader drew a picture.

_____1. "'Ugh!' said Fox. 'Tuna fish!'" ►

_____2. "'<u>Ugh!' said Fox. 'Tuna fish!</u>'"

_____3. "'Ugh!' said Fox. 'Tuna fish!'"► *Why is he saying this?*

_____4. "'Ugh!' said Fox. 'Tuna fish!'"► *I think he will trade lunch with someone else.*

USING YOUR OWN WORDS

Directions: Pick 1 of the ways to be an active reader that you learned about in this lesson. Use your own words to tell what it means.

_____

_____

_____

_____

_____

Writing

COMPLETE SENTENCES

Directions: Mark an X in front of each complete sentence.

_____1. Fox sitting down.

_____2. Tuna fish sandwiches.

_____3. Fox is hungry.

_____4. The happy cat.

_____5. Sandwiches fell from the sky.

WRITING

Directions: Write a complete sentence that describes what happened to Fox's lunch in the story.

_____

- -

_____

- -

_____

- -

_____

- -

_____

- -

_____

- -

_____

Unit Overview

In this unit, students learn what constitutes a good story—engaging characters, a vivid setting, and an exciting plot. Tell students that they will explore how to find clues about a story's characters, how to look for when and where a story takes place, and how to follow a story's plot from beginning to end. Make clear that by understanding these three elements of fiction, students will be on their way to becoming more active readers.

Reading the Art

Be sure students take a moment to "read" the artwork. Have them study the image as they answer these questions:

*   How would you describe the monster and the children?
*   What information do you get from the art?
*   How does the art make you feel?

Literature Focus

Lesson	Literature
1. Character Clues	**Jean Van Leeuwen,** "Growing Up" from *More Tales of Amanda Pig* Amanda and her mother talk about all the wonderful things Amanda will do when she grows up, including becoming a ballet dancer, becoming an astronaut, and building a house next door to her mom's house.
2. Where Are We?	**Cynthia Rylant,** from *Henry and Mudge Under the Yellow Moon* Best friends Henry and Mudge explore the wonders of fall in their own ways.
3. What Is Happening?	**Angela Shelf Medearis,** "The Scary Movie" from *The Adventures of Sugar and Junior* Junior promises Sugar that he'll take care of Sugar at the scary movie, but it ends up that Sugar is much less afraid of the movie than her friend Junior is.

Reading Focus

Lesson	Reading Skill
1. Character Clues	Watch what characters in a story say and do.
2. Where Are We?	As you read, note when and where the story takes place.
3. What Is Happening?	Look for what happens in the beginning, middle, and end of a story.

Writing Focus

Lesson	Writing Assignment
1. Character Clues	Write about the main character and compare her to what you are like.
2. Where Are We?	Draw a picture illustrating the setting of the story. Then describe the setting.
3. What Is Happening?	Tell about something that happened to you and a friend.

1 Character Clues

B e f o r e   R e a d i n g

FOCUS

Watch what characters in a story say and do.

In this lesson, students learn to pay attention to what story characters say and do.

BUILDING BACKGROUND

1. Vocabulary

To make sure students understand the five words below, ask them to complete these **Cloze Sentences.** To begin, write these words on the board. Have students read each word aloud. Ask for a student volunteer to read a sentence with the correct answer.

> ballet   house   live   perfume   midnight

1. On New Year's Eve, Tyler gets to stay up until (*midnight*), but he always falls asleep before then.
2. Amy loves to watch (*ballet*) dancers twirl around the stage.
3. My mom smells sweet when she wears (*perfume*).
4. I (*live*) in a big city with lots of tall buildings.
5. Carlo's family moved into their new (*house*) yesterday.

See **Vocabulary** on page 89 for more practice with these words.

2. Prereading

To help increase students' background for the selection, try this **Think-Pair-and-Share** activity. Ask students to explain what each sentence tells you about Amanda, the main character in the story.

1. "'Mother,' said Amanda. 'What can I do to help you?'"
2. "'I am almost grown up, you know. Soon I will be moving out.'"
3. "Mother and Amanda sat in the big chair."
4. "'I am going to be very busy when I grow up,' said Amanda."
5. "'I will build a house next door to you,' said Amanda."

ADDITIONAL READING

Additional stories for exploring characterization include:

Some Frog! by Eve Bunting (Harcourt Brace and Company, 1998)

Alexander, Who's Not (Do You Hear Me? I Mean It!) Going to Move by Judith Viorst (Atheneum Books for Young Readers, 1995)

D u r i n g   R e a d i n g

FOCUS ON SKILLS

1. Active Reading

Students are asked to underline what Amanda says or does.

Sample Response:

"Mother and Amanda sat in the big chair."

2. Critical Reading Focus

In this lesson, students are asked to focus on what they learned about Amanda based on what she says and does. Understanding characters is critical for students' understanding of a selection as a whole; characters' motivations and characteristics are at the heart of most fiction stories. Examining what characters say and do helps students begin to understand why they act in certain ways.

During | *Reading*

FOCUS ON THE SELECTION

Focus on key passages in the selection to make the point that you learn about characters by paying attention to what they say and do. Help students then make inferences from these observations.

"Growing Up" from ***More Tales of Amanda Pig***
by Jean Van Leeuwen

Ask students,"What is Amanda doing? What do you learn about Amanda here?"

Page 14

"Mother," said Amanda. "What can I do to help you?"

"You can help mix up these muffins for dinner," said mother.

Amanda helped mix up the muffins.

"What a good helper you are getting to be," said Mother.

Ask students,"What does Amanda say? What do you learn about Amanda here?"

Page 15

"I can do a lot of things," said Amanda. "I am almost grown up, you know. Soon I will be moving out."

Ask students,"What does Amanda say? What do you learn about Amanda from what she said?"

Page 16

"I am going to be very busy when I grow up," said Amanda.

"Where will you live," asked Mother, "when you are not on the moon?"

"I will build a house next door to you," said Amanda.

"And I will do whatever I want whenever I want to do it. I will wear perfume all the time and go to bed at midnight and never eat eggs."

Help students to make inferences about characters by discussing what you can learn from a particular action or statement. For example, the above passages show that Amanda has a close relationship with her mother, is eager to grow up, likes to help out, and so on. After you walk students through these parts of the reading, ask them to find other places where Amanda says or does something. Then have them tell what they learned about Amanda from those specific parts of the story.

Explain to students that they will need to find details of what a character says and does in a story to back up their opinions. For instance, if they think Amanda is funny, then ask them to point out where Amanda says or does something funny.

A f t e r | *R e a d i n g*

DISCUSSING THE LITERATURE
Talk about the story with students to help assess their comprehension and understanding of characterization by asking questions such as:
1. Why does Amanda's mother think she is a good helper? (*Amanda helps her make muffins.*)
2. Does Amanda like eggs? What clues in the story help you know this about her? (*No. She says that when she grows up, she will never eat eggs.*)
3. Do you think Amanda is moving out soon? Why or why not? (*Possible: Amanda is still little.*)

REREADING
After students have finished reading, encourage them to go back over the selection. Ask them to look for details of what Amanda says and does that they may not have noticed or underlined before.

See **Comprehension** on page 90 for more help.

W r i t i n g

QUICK ASSESS
Do students' descriptions:

✔ reflect an understanding of the character?

✔ compare Amanda to themselves?

✔ use sentences that begin with capital letters?

In this lesson, students describe Amanda and compare her to themselves.

WRITING ACTIVITIES

1. What Amanda Says and Does
Students begin to respond to the selection by noting what Amanda says and does and what they learn.
Sample Response:
"What can I do to help?" I learn that Amanda seems nice and likes to spend time with her mom.

2. Listing Words
Students select three words to describe Amanda and three words to describe themselves.
Sample Response:
Amanda: helpful, imaginative, nice; Me: funny, smart, nice

3. Describing Amanda
Students should use their notes to describe Amanda and compare her to what they are like.
Sample Response:
Amanda is a little girl with lots of ideas about what she will do when she grows up. She wants to live in her own house next door to her family. I think a lot about the future, too. But I would like to live in a skyscraper in a big city.

See **Writing** on page 91 for more help.

WRITING REMINDERS
As students write their descriptions, remind them to:
• Start each sentence with a capital letter.
• End each sentence with a period, question mark, or exclamation point.
• Include details of what Amanda is like.

88

Vocabulary

WORDS FROM THE SELECTION

Directions: Draw a line from each word to its meaning.

ballet	make your home in
house	12 o'clock at night
live	a kind of dancing
perfume	place to live in
midnight	sweet smell

WORD STUDY: Compound Words

A compound word is a word made up of 2 smaller words.

whenever = when + ever

Directions: Write the 2 small words in each compound word.

softball = soft + ball

grandma =

sandbox =

ladybug =

inside =

Comprehension

CHECKING UNDERSTANDING

Directions: Read each sentence. Circle "T" if the sentence is **true** or "F" if the sentence is **false**.

T F 1. Amanda wants to move far away from her family.

T F 2. Amanda wants to do lots of things when she grows up.

T F 3. Amanda loves eggs.

T F 4. Amanda does not like perfume.

T F 5. Amanda likes to be with her mother.

RETELLING THE STORY

Directions: Write what Amanda wants on the lines below.

_____

_____

_____

_____

_____

_____

_____

_____

Writing

CAPITAL LETTERS AND PERIODS

Directions: Mark an X in front of each sentence that starts with a capital letter and ends with a period.

_____1. Amanda wants to move far away from her family.

_____2. amanda wants to be a cook and a doctor.

_____3. amanda loves eggs

_____4. Amanda is brave.

_____5. Amanda will be busy

WRITING

Directions: Write a sentence that explains something you might like to do when you grow up.

_____

- -

_____

- -

_____

- -

_____

- -

_____

Where Are We?

Before Reading

FOCUS
As you read, note when and where the story takes place.

In this lesson, students learn to look for clues about when and where a story takes place.

BUILDING BACKGROUND

1. Vocabulary
To be sure students understand key vocabulary words before reading the selection, have them complete this **Matching Definitions** exercise. Write the words and definitions in two columns on the board. Ask students to match them by drawing a line between the word in the left column and its definition in the right column. For added practice, have students think of a sentence for each word.

1. *sniffing* — small animals with brown fur who live in the woods
2. *ground* — gathered with your hands
3. *chipmunks* — taking in air through the nose in short breaths
4. *licked* — part of the earth that is hard and made of dirt
5. *picked* — moved the tongue over something

See **Vocabulary** on page 95 for more practice with these words.

2. Prereading
Introduce the selection further by **Previewing** the selection as a whole-class activity. To begin, read aloud the first paragraph on page 20. Then have students look over the illustrations on pages 20 and 21. Discuss the preview by asking students the following questions:
1. Who are the two main characters in the story? (*Henry and Mudge*)
2. What did you learn about these characters from your preview? (*Henry is a boy. Mudge is a dog.*)
3. What do the pictures tell you about the story? (*Mudge likes to eat leaves. Henry and Mudge like apples.*)

ADDITIONAL READING
Additional stories by Cynthia Rylant include:
Henry and Mudge: The First Book of the Adventures (Simon and Schuster, 1996)
Poppleton (Scholastic, 1997)

During Reading

FOCUS ON SKILLS

1. Active Reading
Students are asked to circle words that tell *when* or *where*.
Sample Response:
(Fall) tells when. (Woods) tell where.

2. Critical Reading Focus
In this lesson, students are taught to look for clues that tell them about the setting. Sometimes, the setting is not particularly important, but in stories such as *Henry and Mudge Under the Yellow Moon*, understanding the setting is key to understanding the story as a whole. When the story takes place—fall—affects all the action in the piece.

D u r i n g   R e a d i n g

FOCUS ON THE SELECTION

Focus on key passages in the selection to help students get a clear picture of the setting and the role the setting plays in the story.

from *Henry and Mudge Under the Yellow Moon*
by Cynthia Rylant

Ask students, "What do you learn about when and where the story takes place?"

Ask students, "What clues in the story help you learn more about what the setting looks like?"

Help students see how Cynthia Rylant uses vibrant details to describe not only what the setting looks like, but also what it feels like. Ask students, "What words does Cynthia Rylant use to help you see and feel the setting?"

Help students notice that the author repeats the phrase "in the fall."

Page 20

In the fall, Henry and his big dog Mudge took long walks in the woods.

Henry loved looking at the tops of the trees. He liked the leaves: orange, yellow, brown, and red.

Page 21

Henry put on a coat and Mudge grew one. And when the fall wind blew, Henry's ears turned red and Mudge's ears turned inside out.

Page 22

But one thing about them was the same. In the fall Henry and Mudge liked being together, most of all.

Encourage students to pick out and talk about specific sensory details that help them "see" the setting—for example, the wind blowing, colorful leaves on the ground, and birds in the sky. After you walk students through these parts of the reading, ask them to think of other details Cynthia Rylant could use to describe the setting. Then have them share their reactions to the way the author describes fall in this story.

A f t e r   *R e a d i n g*

DISCUSSING THE LITERATURE
Talk about the story with students to help assess their comprehension and understanding of setting by asking questions such as:

1. What do Henry and Mudge like to do the most in the fall? (*They like to be together.*)
2. What are some things that Henry and Mudge do differently when they walk in the woods? (*Possible: Henry looks at the leaves. Mudge eats them. Henry picks apples, and Mudge licks them.*)
3. What clues in the story let you know that Henry and Mudge like fall? (*Possible: Henry liked counting the birds. Mudge liked watching the chipmunks.*)

REREADING
After students have finished reading the selection, ask them to go back and find new places that give details about the setting.

See **Comprehension** on page 96 for more help.

W r i t i n g

QUICK ASSESS
Do students' descriptions:

✔ accurately describe the setting?

✔ give details that tell when and where the story takes place?

✔ use correct punctuation?

In this lesson, students list words that tell them when and where the story takes place. Then they use these words to draw a picture of and describe the setting.

WRITING ACTIVITIES

1. Words That Tell When and Where
Students begin to respond to the selection by listing words that tell when and where the story takes place.
Sample Response:
fall, birds flying south, fall wind blew, woods

2. Drawing and Describing
Students use their notes about where and when the story takes place to draw a picture of the setting and then describe it in their own words.
Sample Response:

It is fall. Henry and Mudge are walking in the woods. The leaves are changing color. Henry watches birds flying south. It is cold.

See **Writing** on page 97 for more help.

WRITING REMINDERS
As students write their descriptions, remind them to:
• Use their notes from page 22 to help them tell *when* and *where* the story takes place.
• Be sure to use complete sentences.
• Check that each sentence begins with a capital letter and ends with a period, question mark, or exclamation point.

Vocabulary

WORDS FROM THE SELECTION

Directions: Use words from the box to complete each sentence.

| sniffing | ground | chipmunks | licked | picked |

1. I _____ my fingers after eating the popcorn.

2. Steve's dog keeps _____ the muddy

   _____ by the tree.

3. When my mom _____ me up from school

   today, we saw two _____.

WORD STUDY: Suffixes

A suffix is an ending like *-ed* or *-ing*.

Directions: Find the words with the suffixes *-ed* or *-ing* in these sentences. Circle the suffixes.

1. Dogs like catch(ing) balls.

2. The leaves keep falling off the trees.

3. Henry walked in the woods.

4. We picked apples on our field trip.

Comprehension

MAKING A WEB

Directions: Fill in this Web to show what you know about the story's setting. Add 1 detail on each line.

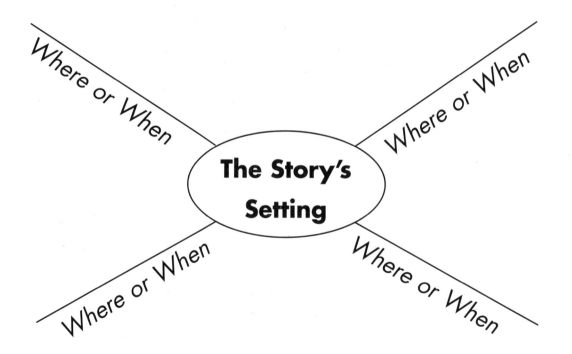

Where or When

Where or When

The Story's Setting

Where or When

Where or When

Writing

COMPLETE SENTENCES

Directions: Mark an X on the line if the sentence begins with a capital letter and ends with a period.

_____1. Henry and Mudge like to take walks.

_____2. In the fall

_____3. putting on a coat.

_____4. Henry picked apples.

_____5. Mudge in the leaves

WRITING

Directions: Write a complete sentence about the setting of *Henry and Mudge Under the Yellow Moon.*

_____

- -

_____

- -

_____

- -

_____

- -

_____

What Is Happening?

Before *Reading*

FOCUS

Look for what happens in the beginning, middle, and end of a story.

In this lesson, students learn that paying attention to what happens in the beginning, middle, and end of a story helps them understand its plot.

BUILDING BACKGROUND

1. Vocabulary

To make sure students understand the five words below, ask them to use **Context Clues** to determine their meaning. Have students read these sentences and then tell what each underlined word means. Ask students what other words would help them understand the meaning.

    tickets   everyone   worry   scared   crawled

1. "Sugar and Junior went to the movies. They paid for their <u>tickets</u>."
2. "'It has lots of monsters in it. But don't be <u>scared</u>, Sugar.'"
3. "'<u>Everyone</u> has left but us.'"
4. "'See?' said Junior as he <u>crawled</u> from under the seat."
5. "'Yes,' Sugar said, 'but don't <u>worry</u>. I'll hold your hand, all the way home.'"

See **Vocabulary** on page 101 for more practice with these words.

2. Prereading

Build more background for the selection by using an **Anticipation Guide**. Ask students to read the three statements below and decide if they agree or disagree with them.

1. Agree   Disagree   Movies with monsters are all scary.
2. Agree   Disagree   Friends help each other.
3. Agree   Disagree   Sometimes people scream when they are scared.

ADDITIONAL READING

Additional stories for exploring plot include:

Why Mosquitoes Buzz in People's Ears: A West African Tale by Verna Aardema (Dial Books, 1975)

The Babe and I by David A. Adler (Harcourt Brace, 1999)

The Father Who Had 10 Children by Benedicte Quettire (Dial Books, 1999)

During *Reading*

FOCUS ON SKILLS

1. Active Reading

Students are asked to write questions about what will happen next.

Sample Response:

Will Sugar scream?

2. Critical Reading Focus

In this lesson, students focus on how the plot of a story develops and keeps the story moving from the beginning to end. Predicting as they read is an excellent activity for remaining focused on the action and connecting events that occur in the beginning, middle, and end of a story.

D u r i n g R e a d i n g

FOCUS ON THE SELECTION

Focus on key passages in the selection to make clear that readers can learn about a story's plot by making predictions as they read.

"The Scary Movie" from *The Adventures of Sugar and Junior*
by Angela Shelf Medearis

Ask students, "What do you learn about the story from how it begins?"

Page 24

"It has lots of monsters in it. But don't be scared, Sugar. I'll hold your hand."

Ask students, "Who do you think is screaming, Junior or Sugar?"

Page 25

Soon the movie started. It was scary. It had lots of monsters. Someone kept screaming and screaming.

Ask students, "What do you think Sugar will do to help Junior?"

Junior hid his face behind his hands. He hid behind the seats. He screamed and he screamed.

Ask students, "What do you think will happen when the movie is over?"

Page 26

"Junior," said Sugar, "please stop screaming. The movie is over. Everyone has left but us."

Ask students, "Do you like the way the story ends?"

"Yes," Sugar said, "but don't worry. I'll hold your hand, all the way home."
   And she did.

After you walk students through these parts of the reading, ask them to look back over their questions. Encourage them to summarize the plot in their own words. Point out that predictions about the plot do not have to be correct in order to be helpful. For example, many students may have predicted that Sugar, not Junior, would be the one who screamed. Review the parts of the story that make readers think Junior will be the brave one. Encourage students to continue thinking about what will happen next when they read stories and to be ready for surprises.

A f t e r R e a d i n g

DISCUSSING THE LITERATURE
Talk about the story with students to help assess their comprehension and understanding of plot by asking questions such as:
1. How does the story begin? (*Junior and Sugar go to a scary movie.*)
2. Do you think Junior is a good friend? Why or why not? (*Possible: Yes, he is a good friend because he tells Sugar that he will take care of her if she is scared.*)
3. Were you surprised by how the story ended? Why or why not? (*Possible: Yes, I thought Junior would have to take care of Sugar.*)

REREADING
After students finish reading the selection, have them go back and reread their questions. Ask them to think about whether the story's ending surprised them.

See **Comprehension** on page 102 for more help.

W r i t i n g

QUICK ASSESS
Do students' stories:

✔ tell about a special time with a friend?

✔ have a clear beginning, middle, and end?

✔ use capital letters for people's names?

In this lesson, students make notes about the story's plot, and then write about something that happened with a friend.

WRITING ACTIVITIES

1. What Happens in the Beginning
Students begin to respond to the selection by noting how the story begins.
Sample Response:

Junior and Sugar go to a scary movie. (beginning)
Junior is scared of the movie. (middle)
Sugar tries to make Junior feel better by holding his hand. (end)

2. Telling a Story
Work with students to brainstorm ideas for their story. After students have decided what they are going to write about, remind them to tell the story from beginning to end.
Sample Response:

My friend Amy lost her dog. She was sad. I helped her look for her dog. We made posters, and we hung them up on trees. We walked around the block. We found Amy's dog. Amy was happy. So was I.

See **Writing** on page 103 for more help.

WRITING REMINDERS
As students tell their stories, remind them to:
*   Write in the first person and use the pronoun *I*.
*   Include what happened first, in the middle, and at the end.
*   Be sure to capitalize people's names.

Vocabulary

WORDS FROM THE SELECTION

Directions: Use the words in the box to fill in the blanks.

tickets	*everyone*	*worry*	*scared*	*crawled*

I saw a scary movie yesterday. The _____ cost $6.00.

I was _____ when the monsters _____ along

the ground. Finally, _____ clapped when the movie

ended. My mom told me not to _____ about monsters.

WORD STUDY: Making New Words

Directions: Use the consonants in the box to build new words. An example has been done for you.

l	s	b	st	gr	d	f	p

Old Word	New Word	Old Word	New Word
1. paid =	laid	4. jump =	
2. real =		5. hand =	
3. meet =		6. mark =	

Comprehension

USING A STORY STRING

Directions: Use this Story String to tell what happens in the beginning, middle, and end of "The Scary Movie."

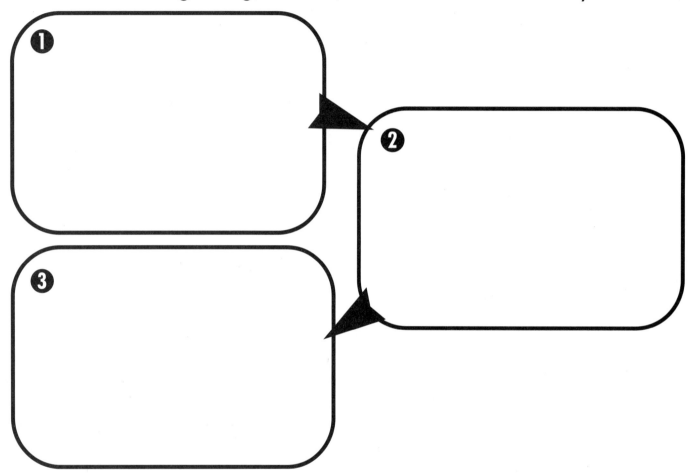

RETELLING THE STORY

Directions: Tell about your favorite part of the story.

_____

Writing

PEOPLE'S NAMES

Directions: Underline all the names of people in these sentences. Then add any capital letters that are missing.

Example: <u>S͟ugar</u> and <u>Junior</u> went to the movies.

1. Junior is a good friend to sugar.

2. Sam thinks monsters can be scary.

3. sugar took good care of junior.

4. junior screamed.

5. My friends rudy and sam like scary movies.

WRITING

Directions: Write a sentence about something you like to do with a friend.

_____

- -

_____

- -

_____

- -

_____

Unit Overview

In this unit, students read nonfiction writing in order to understand the importance of identifying the main idea and supporting details. Explain to students that just by identifying the big, or main, idea of a piece of nonfiction, they can get a jump start on understanding the selection as a whole. Point out that readers can learn a lot about people, places, and events from reading nonfiction. Remind students that nonfiction writing contains facts. Knowing the skills taught in this section will help students better understand and remember the most important facts.

Reading the Art

Ask students to study the art on this page. Then come together as a class to discuss it:

- What does this art show?
- What do you think the boy is doing?
- How would you describe the art?

Literature Focus

Lesson	Literature
1. Looking for the Main Idea	**Allan Fowler,** from *The Sun Is Always Shining Somewhere* In this nonfiction piece, students discover why and how the sun shines all the time, even when it is dark in their part of the Earth.
2. Big Ideas and Small	**Melvin Berger,** from *Germs Make Me Sick!* Readers learn all about germs, from what they look like to where they are found.
3. What's It About?	**Paul Showers,** from *Sleep Is for Everyone* In this engaging nonfiction piece, readers learn about the wide variety of sleeping habits among animals.

Reading Focus

Lesson	Reading Skill
1. Looking for the Main Idea	As you read, look for the main idea.
2. Big Ideas and Small	As you read, sort the big ideas from the details.
3. What's It About?	As you read, ask yourself, "What is the author saying?"

Writing Focus

Lesson	Writing Assignment
1. Looking for the Main Idea	Retell what the selection is about.
2. Big Ideas and Small	Tell the main idea of the selection and one or two supporting details.
3. What's It About?	Use your notes and Web to retell what you learned about sleep.

Looking for the Main Idea

B e f o r e R e a d i n g

FOCUS

As you read, look for the main idea.

In this lesson, students learn to identify the main idea and details in a selection.

BUILDING BACKGROUND

1. Vocabulary

Help students become familiar with the words below with a **Vocabulary Quiz Show**. Write each word on a 3 x 5 index card. Then write a definition for each word on five additional cards. Pass out the cards to ten students. Ask students who have cards with a vocabulary word to say their word aloud. Have the student who has the card with the matching meaning of the word read it aloud. Continue until you are satisfied that students are familiar with all five words.

   shining   pretend   tiny   imagine   light

See **Vocabulary** on page 109 for more practice with these words.

2. Prereading

Provide additional introduction to students by **Previewing** the selection as a group activity. Begin by reading aloud the title. Then encourage students to look over the pictures on pages 30, 31, and 32. To help them organize their preview, ask questions such as:

1. Based on your preview, what do you think this selection is about? (*Possible: It tells why the sun is always shining even when it is dark in my town.*)
2. What clues did the preview give to let you know that this is a piece of nonfiction? (*Possible: One picture looks like an experiment, and another looks like it is explaining something about the sun.*)
3. What do you already know about the sun always shining somewhere? (*Possible: I know that when it is nighttime where I live, it is daytime on the other side of the world.*)

ADDITIONAL READING

Additional stories for exploring main idea include:
The Emperor's Egg by Martin Jenkins (Candlewick Press, 1999)
My Horse of the North by Bruce McMillan (Scholastic, 1997)

D u r i n g R e a d i n g

FOCUS ON SKILLS

1. Active Reading

Students are asked to mark the most important idea and two or three details.
Sample Response:
"Earth is like a ball—a very big ball. It is always turning."

2. Critical Reading Focus

In this lesson, students explore the importance of identifying the main idea and supporting details in a nonfiction selection. Finding the main idea is critical to understanding any piece of nonfiction. But identifying the main idea can be tricky, particularly when it is not as clearly stated as in this selection. Providing consistent practice in identifying the main idea and supporting details from the earliest grades will empower students with this fundamental reading skill. One important first step is teaching students to identify the subject of the paragraph. Then ask students what the writer is saying about the subject.

D u r i n g | *R e a d i n g*

FOCUS ON THE SELECTION
Focus on key passages in the selection to make clear how readers can identify the main idea and supporting details of a nonfiction selection.

Point out to students that this sentence contains the main idea of the selection. Have students note how similar it is to the title of the piece. Explain that titles can often provide clues about a selection's main idea.

Make clear that this paragraph gives important details about the main idea. Ask students, "Why is it important to know that the Earth is always turning?"

Point out that sometimes the main idea is repeated at the end of a selection.

from *The Sun Is Always Shining Somewhere*
by Allan Fowler

Page 30

The sun never stops shining.

Page 31

Earth is like a ball—a very big ball. It is always turning.

Even when you're asleep at night, the sun is always shining—somewhere.

After you walk students through these parts of the reading, ask them to look for more details that tell them about the main idea—the sun is always shining. Come together as a class and invite students to share their details. Work with students to help them distinguish between important details and less essential information.

Talk with students about how they can keep track of what they're reading about. For instance, fill out and talk about a simple Main Idea and Details Organizer as a model.

Main Idea: The sun is always shining somewhere.		
Detail 1	**Detail 2**	**Detail 3**
The Earth is like a ball.	The Earth is always turning.	When it's night in one part of the world, it's daylight somewhere else.

A f t e r R e a d i n g

DISCUSSING THE LITERATURE
Talk about the selection with students to help assess their comprehension of the selection and understanding of main ideas by asking questions such as:
1. What is the most important idea of the selection? (*The sun is always shining somewhere.*)
2. How can you tell which details are most important? (*They should tell me more about the main idea.*)
3. Were you surprised by anything you learned in this selection? (*Possible: I didn't know that the Earth is always turning.*)

REREADING
After students finish reading the selection, ask them to review the places they marked. Encourage them to mark details they might not have picked out before.

See **Comprehension** on page 110 for more help.

W r i t i n g

QUICK ASSESS
Do students' retellings:

✔ begin with the main idea?

✔ include supporting details?

✔ use proper end punctuation?

In this lesson, students continue working on finding the main idea by writing down the most important sentence and then retelling the selection in their own words.

WRITING ACTIVITIES

1. What the Reading Is About
Students begin to respond to the selection by identifying the key topics and main idea.
Sample Response:

sun, Earth; "The sun never stops shining."

2. Retelling the Selection
Students finish responding to the selection by retelling it in their own words.
Sample Response:

The Sun Is Always Shining Somewhere tells about how even when it is dark in my city, it is sunny on the other part of the world. The Earth is always turning. It is daytime in my city when my part of the Earth turns toward the sun. It is nighttime in my city when the Earth turns away from the sun. Even when I sleep, it is sunny somewhere else.

See **Writing** on page 111 for more help.

WRITING REMINDERS
As students retell the selection, remind them to:
• Begin with the main idea of the selection.
• Use their own words to retell key details.
• Reread their writing to make sure they spelled each word correctly and used proper end punctuation.

Vocabulary

WORDS FROM THE SELECTION

Directions: Read each sentence from the story. Then tell what the underlined word means.

1. "The sun never stops <u>shining</u>."

I think <u>shining</u> means _____.

2. "<u>Pretend</u> the mark is you."

I think <u>pretend</u> means _____.

3. "Put a <u>tiny</u> mark on a ball."

I think <u>tiny</u> means _____.

4. "<u>Imagine</u> the ball is the Earth."

I think <u>imagine</u> means _____.

WORD STUDY: Suffixes

A suffix is a part added to the end of a base word.

Directions: Add suffixes to these words to make new words. An example has been done for you.

1. turn + ing = turning

2. back + ward =

3. pretend + ed =

4. teach + er =

Comprehension

LISTING THE MAIN IDEA AND DETAILS

Directions: Fill in the circle with the main idea of *The Sun Is Always Shining Somewhere.* Write 1 detail about the main idea on each of the lines.

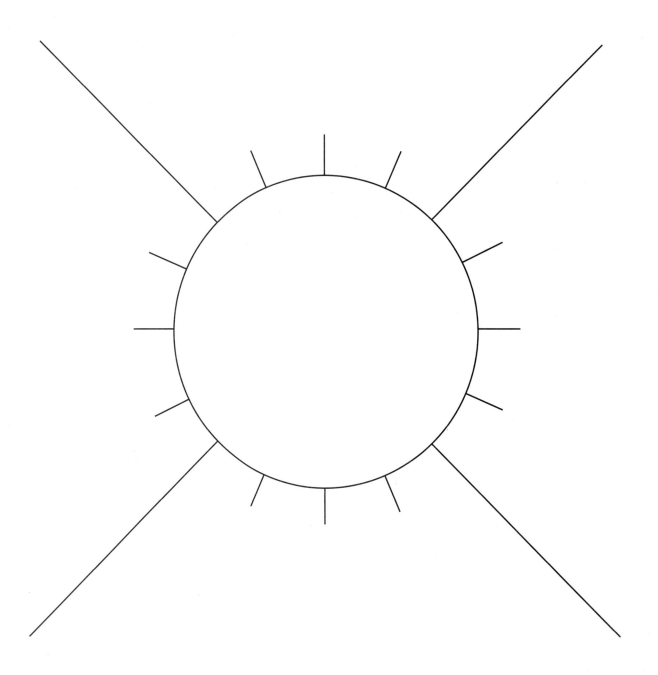

Writing

PERIODS AND QUESTION MARKS

Directions: Add a . (period) or ? (question mark) to finish each sentence.

1. The sun always shines somewhere

2. Did you know that the Earth is always turning

3. Why does the sun set at night

4. How is the Earth like a big ball

5. I did not know that the sun is always shining

WRITING

Directions: Write a sentence about what you learned from this selection. Then write a question you have about the selection.

1. Sentence:

_____

_____

_____

2. Question:

_____

_____

_____

2 Big Ideas and Small

B e f o r e   R e a d i n g

In this lesson, students continue working on identifying the main idea and supporting details when reading nonfiction.

BUILDING BACKGROUND

1. Vocabulary

To be sure students understand key vocabulary words before reading the selection, have them complete this **Vocabulary Inventory**. Have students write the following words on a piece of paper:

> *ache   germ   bacteria   viruses   microscope*

Then have students place a mark next to each word to indicate how well they know it (+ = know this word, ? = seems familiar, 0 = don't know this word). After students complete the inventory, come together as a class and discuss their markings. Encourage students to make predictions about what the selection will be about based on these key vocabulary words.

See **Vocabulary** on page 115 for more practice with these words.

2. Prereading

Provide additional introduction to students by using an **Anticipation Guide**. First, have students circle whether they agree or disagree with each statement. As a class, discuss their answers. Return to the activity after reading to see if students' answers change.

1. Agree   Disagree   Germs are everywhere.
2. Agree   Disagree   Germs are tiny living things.
3. Agree   Disagree   You can see germs in the air.

ADDITIONAL READING

Additional selections for exploring main ideas include:

Why I Sneeze, Shiver, Hiccup, and Yawn by Melvin Berger (HarperCollins, 2000)
Terrible Tyrannosaurs by Kathleen Zoehfield (HarperCollins, 2001)

D u r i n g   R e a d i n g

FOCUS ON SKILLS

1. Active Reading

Students are asked to mark and write one detail on each page.
Sample Response:

Germs are very small living things.

2. Critical Reading Focus

In this lesson, students continue exploring the importance of identifying the main idea and supporting details of a nonfiction selection. Nonfiction reading material can bombard readers with hundreds of words and ideas. The ability to separate essential ideas from smaller ones is crucial for understanding and retaining key information in informational text. Sorting out these details can be difficult for some students. One technique that might help them is to ask students to stop after each paragraph and ask themselves, "What is this all about?"

During Reading

FOCUS ON THE SELECTION

Focus on key passages in the selection to make the make clear how readers can identify the main idea and supporting details of a nonfiction selection.

from *Germs Make Me Sick!*
by Melvin Berger

Point out that this paragraph contains lots of information about germs. Ask students, "Which facts do you think are most important to remember? Why?"

Page 34

Germs are tiny living things. They are far too small to see with your eyes alone. In fact, a line of one thousand germs could fit across the top of a pencil!

Point out that as students continue to read, they should look for more information about bacteria and viruses.

Page 35

There are many different kinds of germs. But the two that usually make you sick are bacteria and viruses.

Again, point out that this paragraph contains lots of facts about viruses. Talk with students about how they decide which facts are most important to remember.

Viruses are far tinier than bacteria. Some look like balls with spikes sticking out on all sides. Others look like loaves of bread or like tadpoles. There are even some that look like metal screws with spider legs.

Ask students, "What is the most important fact you learned from reading this paragraph?"

Page 36

Germs, such as bacteria and viruses, are found everywhere. They are in the air you breathe, in the food you eat, in the water you drink, and on everything you touch. They are even on your skin and in your body.

As you walk students through these parts of the reading, help them distinguish between important details and less essential information. For instance, as you review the last paragraph on page 35, be sure students understand that the most important point is that viruses are small and come in all different shapes. The descriptions of spikes, tadpoles, and spider legs are less important specific details.

A f t e r   *R e a d i n g*

DISCUSSING THE LITERATURE
Talk about the story with students to help assess their comprehension and understanding of main idea and supporting details by asking questions such as:
1. What is the most important idea of the selection? (*Germs make you sick.*)
2. What fact did you find most interesting? Why? (*Possible: Germs are everywhere.*)
3. How can you decide what facts are most important when you read nonfiction? (*Possible: They should tell me more about the main idea.*)

REREADING
After students finish reading the selection, encourage them to reread it. Ask them to be sure they have circled the main ideas on each page, and encourage them to make any changes they want.

See **Comprehension** on page 116 for more help.

W r i t i n g

QUICK ASSESS
Do students' paragraphs:

✓ begin with the main idea?

✓ include supporting details?

✓ use complete sentences?

In this lesson, students identify the main idea and three details that support the main idea. They then write a paragraph telling what they learned from the selection.

WRITING ACTIVITIES

1. The Main Idea
Students begin to respond to the selection by identifying what the reading is about.
Sample Response:
It is about how germs make you sick.

2. Three Details
Students continue responding to the selection by listing three details that support the main idea.
Sample Response:
1. Germs are tiny living things.
2. There are two kinds of germs that make you sick.
3. Germs are everywhere.

3. Telling What You Learned
Students write a paragraph about what they learned.
Sample Response:
I learned that germs can make me sick. There are lots of different kinds of germs. Bacteria and viruses are germs that can make me sick. Germs are everywhere. They are even on me!

See **Writing** on page 117 for more help.

WRITING REMINDERS
As students tell what they learned, remind them to:
- Include the main idea and one or two details.
- Use complete sentences.
- Check to see that each sentence begins with a capital letter and ends with a period, question mark, or exclamation point.

Vocabulary

WORDS FROM THE SELECTION

Directions: Use the words below to complete each sentence.

| ache | bacteria | viruses | microscope |

1. Two kinds of germs are _____ and _____.

2. My arms and legs _____ when I have the flu.

3. A _____ helps you see tiny things.

WORD STUDY: Syllables

Directions: Read the words in the box. Write each word. Then draw a line between the consonants in the middle.

| getting | pencil | tadpole | inside |

get/ting

_____

_____

_____

Comprehension

UNDERSTANDING THE MAIN IDEA AND DETAILS

Directions: Fill in the chart to organize what you learned from reading *Germs Make Me Sick!*

Main Idea

Detail

Detail

Detail

Writing

COMPLETE SENTENCES

Directions: Match words from column A with words from column B to make complete sentences. Write the sentences on the lines.

Column A	Column B
1. Germs can	two kinds of germs.
2. Bacteria and viruses are	in all kinds of shapes.
3. Germs come	make people sick.

3 **What's It About?**

B e f o r e | *R e a d i n g*

FOCUS

As you read, ask yourself, "What is the author saying?"

In this lesson, students learn how to determine the author's message.

BUILDING BACKGROUND

1. Vocabulary

To help students with the selection's vocabulary, ask them to complete these **Cloze Sentences**. To begin, ask a volunteer to read a sentence with the correct vocabulary word added. After completing the activity, have students make up new sentences using these words for other students to complete:

| eyelids | pigeon | lie | curl | elephant |

1. "Sometimes dogs (_curl_) up."
2. "A (_pigeon_) sits down when it sleeps."
3. "Snakes have no (_eyelids_)."
4. "Pigs (_lie_) down to sleep."
5. "An (_elephant_) can sleep standing up."

See **Vocabulary** on page 121 for more practice with these words.

2. Prereading

Give students more introduction to the selection by **Previewing** it as a whole class. Read aloud the first paragraph. Then have students look at the picture on the bottom of page 38. Here are some questions to discuss:

1. What did you learn from the first paragraph of the selection? (*Possible: Animals sleep in different ways.*)
2. What did you learn from the illustration? (*Possible: Snakes keep their eyes open when they sleep.*)
4. Based on what you learned from the preview and the vocabulary activity, what do you think the selection will be about? (*Possible: I think the selection will be about the different ways animals sleep.*)

ADDITIONAL READING

Additional selections by Paul Showers include:
Hear Your Heart (HarperCollins, 2001)
What Happens to a Hamburger? (HarperCollins, 2001)
Where Does the Garbage Go? (HarperCollins, 1994)

D u r i n g | *R e a d i n g*

FOCUS ON SKILLS

1. Active Reading

Students are asked to write one important point that they would tell someone on each page.
Sample Response:

Snakes don't have eyelids.

2. Critical Reading Focus

In this lesson, students explore the importance of understanding the author's message. Identifying what the author has to say about a subject will enable students to better understand the main idea of the selection and also to remember important facts.

D u r i n g   R e a d i n g

FOCUS ON THE SELECTION

Focus on key passages in the selection to help students see how they can recognize what the author has to say about a subject.

from *Sleep Is for Everyone*
by Paul Showers

Ask students, "What is Paul Showers trying to get you to think about?"

Point out that this short piece contains many facts about sleep. Talk with students about ways they can remember these facts.

Page 38

When you go to sleep, which way do your eyelids go?

Page 39

Sometimes dogs curl up. So do cats. Cows don't. Do you?

After you walk students through these parts of the reading, ask them to work with a partner to answer the two questions Paul Showers asks them on pages 38 and 39. Be sure that students understand that Showers talks about two aspects of how humans and various animals sleep: what their eyes do and what position their body is in. Point out details (about the different kinds of animals) so students can see how they all relate to the big idea (sleep).

You may want to work together to make a Web to keep track of what the author is saying about a subject. Here is one example you could draw.

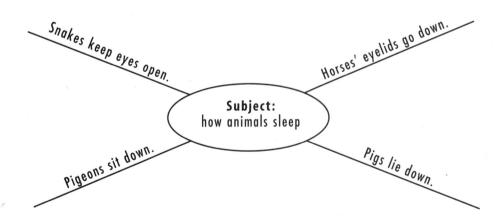

Snakes keep eyes open.

Horses' eyelids go down.

Subject: how animals sleep

Pigeons sit down.

Pigs lie down.

A f t e r | *R e a d i n g*

DISCUSSING THE LITERATURE
Talk with students to help assess their comprehension and understanding of the selection by asking questions such as:
1. What is this selection all about? (*It is about the different ways animals and people sleep.*)
2. Why do you think Paul Showers gave so many different examples of how animals sleep? (*Possible: He wants to show us all the different ways there are to sleep.*)
3. What is the one way to remember what an author says? (*Possible: Retell what you read in your own words.*)

REREADING
After students finish reading the selection, have them go back and review the notes they made. Encourage them to reread and to share what they wrote with a partner and talk about any differences.

See **Comprehension** on page 122 for more help.

W r i t i n g

In this lesson, students first write three facts from the selection in a Web and then use their response notes and Web to tell what they learned about sleep.

WRITING ACTIVITIES

1. Making a Web
Students begin to respond to the selection by listing three ways animals sleep.
Sample Response:
1. Pigs lie down.
2. Dogs curl up.
3. Snakes keep their eyes open.

2. Telling What You Learned
Students continue responding to the selection by writing an important fact from each page in their own words.
Sample Response:
1. Snakes sleep with their eyes open.
2. Cows do not curl up when they sleep.

See **Writing** on page 123 for more help.

WRITING REMINDERS
As students list their facts, remind them to:
- Write a fact from each page.
- Use complete sentences.
- Check to see that they spelled each word correctly.

Vocabulary

WORDS FROM THE SELECTION

Directions: Use the words in the word box to fill in the blanks.

eyelids   pigeon   lie   curl   elephant

What I Learned About Sleep

1. Did you know that snakes have no _____ ?

2. Cats and dogs like to _____ up when the sleep.

3. Pigs like to _____ down.

4. A _____ sits down when it sleeps, but an

_____ sleeps standing up.

WORD STUDY: Compound Words

You can make a compound word by joining two small ones.

base + ball = baseball

Directions: Make compound words by drawing a line from a word in Column A to a word in Column B.

Column A	Column B
some	ball
foot	times
with	out

Name ....

Comprehension

WRITING THE MAIN IDEA AND DETAILS

Directions: Fill in the most important idea from *Sleep Is for Everyone* in the eyeball. List 5 facts on the lines.

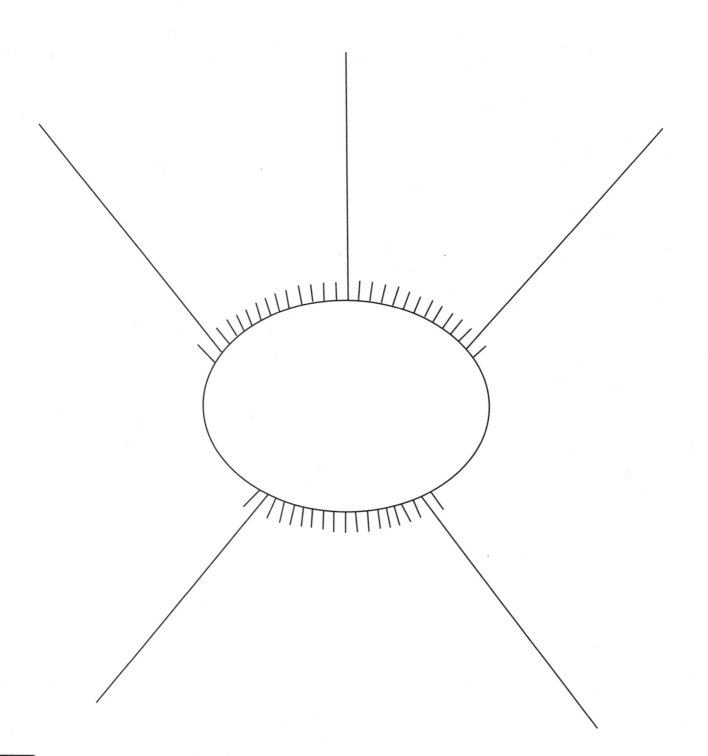

Writing

SPELLING

Directions: Circle the 1 word in each sentence that is <u>not</u> spelled correctly.

1. Pigs sleap too.
2. Did you no about sleep?
3. Wat do you do when you sleep?
4. Pigs lye down to sleep.
5. I kurl up when I sleep.

WRITING

Directions: Pick 3 of the words that were not spelled correctly. Write a sentence using each of these words. Make sure you check the spelling of each word.

1.

2.

3.

Unit Overview

In this unit, students explore the work of three writers: Wade Hudson, Jama Kim Rattigan, and Arnold Lobel. As they read the stories in this section, students will discover how authors create memorable characters, how they choose their words, and why they include a problem in the plot of their stories. Point out to students that every writer has a different way of writing. This is called their "style." Encourage students to think about each author's style as they read the stories in this unit.

Reading the Art

Ask students to look carefully at the art on this page. Then discuss the following questions as a whole-class activity:

- What clues do you get from the art about the stories in this section?
- Which image interests you the most? Why?
- What can you tell about the boy from his picture?

L i t e r a t u r e   F o c u s

Lesson	Literature
1. Learning About Characters	**Wade Hudson,** from *Jamal's Busy Day* Jamal describes all the things he and his family do during their busy day.
2. Authors Choose Words	**Jama Kim Rattigan,** from *Truman's Aunt Farm* Truman is in for quite a surprise when his Aunt Fran sends him a special birthday gift.
3. What a Problem!	**Arnold Lobel,** from "The Wishing Well" A smart mouse figures out an ingenious way to solve her problem and makes all her wishes come true.

R e a d i n g   F o c u s

Lesson	Reading Skill
1. Learning About Characters	Note what the characters in a story are like and what they say and do.
2. Authors Choose Words	Notice the words a writer uses in a story.
3. What a Problem!	Look for the problem and how it's solved in a story.

W r i t i n g   F o c u s

Lesson	Writing Assignment
1. Learning About Characters	Tell how Jamal acts in the beginning, middle, and end of the story.
2. Authors Choose Words	Write a letter to Truman's aunt telling her what you think of the story so far.
3. What a Problem!	Make a book cover that illustrates the mouse's problem and how she solves it.

Learning About Characters

FOCUS

Note what the characters in a story are like and what they say and do.

In this lesson, students learn how authors create memorable characters.

BUILDING BACKGROUND

1. Vocabulary

To give students help with some of the words from the selection, use this **Matching Definitions** activity. To begin, write these two columns on the board. Ask student volunteers to draw a line from the word in the left column to its definition in the right column. For added practice, ask students to think of a sentence for each word.

1. *architect*   a person who watches over and directs others
2. *accountant*   tests a person does to see what happens
3. *experiments*   a person who takes care of money
4. *research*   a person who designs buildings
5. *supervisor*   a study to find and learn more facts

See **Vocabulary** on page 129 for more practice with these words.

2. Prereading

Use this **Think-Pair-and-Share** activity to get students ready to read the selection. Ask students to read these sentences from the story and then predict what it will be about.

1. "Mommy, Daddy and I start our work day early."
2. "Before we leave for work, we eat a healthy breakfast."
3. "The bus is always crowded."
4. "Sometimes I bring work home."
5. "Later, Daddy and Mommy talk about their busy day."

ADDITIONAL READING

Additional stories by Wade Hudson include:

Afro-bets Book of Black Heroes from A to Z: An Introduction to Important Black Achievers for Young Readers (Just Us Books, 1988)

Robo's Favorite Places (Just Us Books, 1991)

Pass It On: African-American Poetry for Children (Scholastic, 1993)

D u r i n g   R e a d i n g

FOCUS ON SKILLS

1. Active Reading

Students are asked to write questions about the characters.

Sample Response:

What kind of work clothes does Jamal wear?

2. Critical Reading Focus

Most stories revolve around characters—how they look, act, think, talk, and interact with one another. The ability to get underneath a character's skin to truly get a sense of what he or she is all about empowers proficient readers and motivates reluctant readers to continue reading. Curiosity about characters and what they'll do next keeps us turning pages.

D u r i n g | *R e a d i n g*

FOCUS ON THE SELECTION

Focus on key passages in the selection to make clear how readers can learn about characters by paying attention to how they act, think, and feel.

from *Jamal's Busy Day*
by Wade Hudson

Ask students, "What do you learn about Jamal and his family from this paragraph?"

Page 42

Before we leave for work, we eat a healthy breakfast. We have to be ready for our busy day.

Point out that in these two paragraphs, readers learn much about Jamal's dad and mom. They also learn about Jamal. Ask, "What do you learn about Jamal from what he thinks about his mom and dad?"

Page 43

My daddy is an architect. He makes drawings to guide the people who build houses. He works hard.

My mommy is an accountant. She's always busy with numbers. Mommy works very hard.

Ask students, "What do you learn about Jamal from how he describes his day?"

Page 44

My supervisor always calls on me for a helping hand. And sometimes I have to settle disagreements between my co-workers. There is always work to do.

Getting home is not easy, either. The bus is always crowded. But when I get there, I relax. I have to unwind.

Ask students, "What does Jamal do at the end of his day? What does this tell you about him?"

Page 45

Then I shoot a few hoops. Soon, it's time for dinner. We all help. I set the table.

Later, Daddy and Mommy talk about their busy day. I say, "I know just what you mean. I've had a busy day myself."

Help students recognize the character clues in the above passages. For instance, point out that Jamal seems to have a close family; he and his parents enjoy eating breakfast and dinner together and talking about their days. After you walk students through these parts of the reading, ask students to find other places where they learn about Jamal and his family. Then have students tell what they learned about the characters in the story from these additional details.

A f t e r   R e a d i n g

DISCUSSING THE LITERATURE
Talk about the story with students to help assess their comprehension and understanding of characterization by asking questions such as:
1. What kind of work does Jamal do? (*He goes to school.*)
2. What do you learn about Jamal by how he describes his work? (*Possible: He takes his work very seriously.*)
3. Would you like to be Jamal's friend? Why or why not? (*Possible: Yes, because I like to play basketball too.*)

REREADING
After students finish reading the selection, have them review the questions that they wrote. Ask them to reread the story and, as they do, to think about possible answers to them.

See **Comprehension** on page 130 for more help.

W r i t i n g

QUICK ASSESS
Do students' descriptions of Jamal's actions:

✔ show an understanding of what happens in the story?

✔ mention at least three things Jamal does in the story?

In this lesson, students write about three things Jamal does in the story.

WRITING ACTIVITIES

1. What Jamal Does in the Beginning
Students begin to respond to the selection by telling what Jamal does in the beginning of the story.
Sample Response:
Jamal brushes his teeth and eats breakfast.

2. What Jamal Does in the Middle
Students continue responding to the selection by describing what Jamal does in the middle of the story.
Sample Response:
Jamal goes to school.

3. What Jamal Does in the End
Students finish responding to the selection by describing what Jamal does at the end of the story.
Sample Response:
Jamal talks to his mom and dad about his busy day.

See **Writing** on page 131 for more help.

WRITING REMINDERS
As students tell about Jamal, remind them to:
• Use their own words.
• Start each sentence with a capital letter.
• Reread their writing to make sure they spelled each word correctly and used proper punctuation.

Vocabulary

WORDS FROM THE SELECTION

Directions: Read this diary entry. Fill in the blanks with words from the word box.

architect	accountant	experiments	research	supervisor

Dear Diary,

Today, I did a few _____ to see what happens

when you put an egg in water. I love doing _____

on all kinds of things. I sometimes pretend that my teacher is my

_____, and I am a scientist. My mom works with

money. She is an _____. My dad plans buildings.

He is an _____. I am going to sleep now so that I

can be ready for work tomorrow.

Comprehension

UNDERSTANDING A CHARACTER

Directions: Read what Jamal does, thinks, or says in the left-hand column. Tell what you learn about Jamal in the right-hand column.

Double-entry Journal

What Jamal Does, Thinks, or Says	What This Means About Jamal
"Then I shoot a few hoops."	
"We all help. I set the table."	
"But I can't wait until tomorrow."	

Writing

USING YOUR OWN WORDS

Directions: When you retell a story, it is important to use your own words. Rewrite these sentences from the story in your own words.

Example: "Mommy, Daddy, and I start our work day early."

Jamal and his family get up early.

1. "Before we leave for work, we eat a healthy breakfast."

_____

- -

_____

- -

_____

2. "I have to unwind."

_____

- -

_____

- -

_____

3. "And sometimes I have to settle disagreements between my co-workers."

_____

- -

_____

- -

_____

Authors Choose Words

Before Reading

FOCUS

Notice the words a writer uses in a story.

In this lesson, students learn how authors use words to express themselves.

BUILDING BACKGROUND

1. Vocabulary

Use this **Context Clues** activity to help students understand key vocabulary words from the selection. Read aloud each sentence below. Ask students to use context clues to determine the meaning of the underlined words.

   package   aunts   fuss   nephew   subscriptions

1. "At eleven o'clock a <u>package</u> arrived for Truman. It was a birthday present from Aunt Fran."
2. "But he didn't get ants. He got <u>aunts</u>."
3. "They all loved Truman and made such a <u>fuss</u>!"
4. "Love, Your bug-loving <u>nephew</u>, Truman."
5. "They brought their knitting and homemade banana bread and gave Truman more than one hundred-something gift <u>subscriptions</u> to children's magazines."

See **Vocabulary** on page 135 for more practice with these words.

2. Prereading

Provide readiness for the selection by **Previewing** the selection as a group activity. Begin by reading aloud the title. Then have students read the first page of the story. Come together as a class to discuss these questions:

1. Who is the story about? (*a boy named Truman*)
2. What clues does the title give you about what the story will be about? (*It is about an aunt farm, not an ant farm.*)
3. What do you learn about Aunt Fran from the first page of the story? (*Possible: She gives interesting presents.*)

ADDITIONAL READING

Additional stories by Jama Kim Rattigan include:
The Woman in the Moon: A Story from Hawai'i (Little Brown and Co. 1996)
Dumpling Soup (Little Brown and Co. 1998)

During Reading

FOCUS ON SKILLS

1. Active Reading

Students are asked to circle one or two descriptive words on each page of the selection.
Sample Response:
gently, yellow

2. Critical Reading Focus

In this lesson, students learn to identify the interesting words and details that make up an author's style. Understanding an author's style enables readers to better appreciate the various ways an author can use words to express his or her ideas.

D u r i n g   R e a d i n g

FOCUS ON THE SELECTION
Focus on key passages in the selection to make clear how authors choose words carefully to express themselves.

from *Truman's Aunt Farm*
by Jama Kim Rattigan

Point out to students that in this very first paragraph, Jama Kim Rattigan uses a number of words to describe what Truman does with the box. Ask students to list some of these key words.

Page 47

At eleven o'clock a package arrived for Truman. It was a birthday present from Aunt Fran. Truman looked at the box. It was not moving. He gently picked it up. It felt empty. He turned it over, then smelled it. Presents from Aunt Fran had to be handled very carefully.

Point out how the author's word play (*ants* versus *aunts*) sets the stage for the rest of the story's fun.

Page 48

But he didn't get ants. He got aunts.

Discuss together what the phrase "talked his ears off" means and why the author might have used such an unusual phrase.

Page 49

"Looks just like me," said Aunt Ramona. And they hugged him, and patted his head, and pinched his cheeks, and talked his ears off.

Ask students, "What do you learn about the aunts here?"

Page 50

Truman looked out his front window. A long, long line of aunts was waiting to get in. They brought their knitting and homemade banana bread and gave Truman more than one hundred-something gift subscriptions to children's magazines.

Point out the sentence, "Don't let those ants bug you." Help students see the author's clever choice of words here.

Page 51

My dear Truman,
I am glad you liked the present. Don't let those ants bug you. Do you have any friends who would like some ants?

After you walk students through these parts of the reading, ask them to look for more examples of the way Jama Kim Rattigan chooses words to help make her writing special. Encourage them to share opinions about what they like about her style.

A f t e r   R e a d i n g

DISCUSSING THE LITERATURE
Talk about the story with students to help assess their comprehension and understanding of word choice by asking questions such as:
1. How does this story make you feel? Why? (*Possible: It makes me feel good because it is so funny.*)
2. Do you think the author's choice of words helped you feel this way? (*Possible: I think the words she used made the story funnier than it would have been if she chose different words.*)
3. What did you like the best about the story? (*Possible: I liked when the aunts started lining up outside Truman's house.*)

REREADING
After students finish reading the selection, have them go back and review their circled words. Ask them to circle any other interesting words they find as they reread.

See **Comprehension** on page 136 for more help.

W r i t i n g

QUICK ASSESS
Do students' letters:

✓ make clear what they think of the story?

✓ demonstrate an understanding of the story?

✓ show creativity?

In this lesson, students first list their favorite words from the story. Then they write their own letter to Aunt Fran.

WRITING ACTIVITIES

1. Favorite Words
Students begin to respond to the selection by listing the three words that they liked the best and why they liked them.
Sample Response:
I liked <u>charming</u> because I like the way it sounds.

2. Writing a Letter
Students continue responding to the selection by writing a letter to Aunt Fran in which they tell what they think of the story so far.
Sample Response:
Dear Aunt Fran,
    I think this story is funny. I like how the aunts showed up instead of ants. Truman is lucky to have you give him such a surprise.

See **Writing** on page 137 for more help.

WRITING REMINDERS
As students write their letters, remind them to:
*   Begin all names with capital letters.
*   Use complete sentences.
*   Reread their writing to make sure they spelled each word correctly and used proper punctuation.

Vocabulary

WORDS FROM THE SELECTION

Directions: Read the letter. Fill in the blanks with words from the word box.

nephew	aunts	subscription	package	fuss

Dear Tyler,

I can't wait to tell you about the _____

I got on my birthday. It was from two of my _____.

Aunt Sophie and Aunt Sarah always make such a

_____ over me. They say I am their favorite

_____. The present was wrapped in a big

square box. I was sure it was a new toy. But when I opened it, I

was surprised to find a _____ to my favorite

magazine. I was so happy.

Your friend,

Andy

Comprehension

THINKING ABOUT WORDS

Directions: Read the lines from the story in the first column. Tell how the words make you feel in the second column.

Double-entry Journal

Lines from the Story	How the Words Make Me Feel
"Presents from Aunt Fran had to be handled very carefully."	
"'Watch them work! Watch them play! Watch them eat! Live ants!'"	
"Love, Your bug-loving nephew, Truman"	

Writing

CORRECTING A LETTER

Directions: There are 6 mistakes in this letter. Can you spot them all? Circle the mistakes. Then rewrite the letter without the mistakes.

Deer Aunt Linda,

Thanks for the hamster

I named him spot. Do you like that name.

Dad thinks he is going to be a great Friend.

Love,

michael

What a Problem!

B e f o r e   *R e a d i n g*

FOCUS

Look for the problem and how it's solved in a story.

In this lesson, students learn how to identify the problem and how it is solved in a story.

BUILDING BACKGROUND

1. Vocabulary

wishes	*found*	*well*	*ouch*	*true*

Help students become familiar with the above words using a **Vocabulary Quiz Show**. Write each word on a 3 x 5 index card. Then write a definition for each word on five additional cards. Pass out the cards to ten students. Ask student volunteers to say their word aloud. Have the student who has the card with the meaning of the word read it aloud. Continue until you are satisfied that students are familiar with all five words.

See **Vocabulary** on page 141 for more practice with these words.

2. Prereading

To help activate students' prior knowledge, create a **Word Web** around the phrase *wishing well*. Have students share their ideas.

ADDITIONAL READING

Additional stories by Arnold Lobel include:
Ming Lo Moves the Mountain (Mulberry Books, 1982)
Owl at Home (HarperCollins, 1987)
Frog and Toad Together (HarperCollins, 1972)

D u r i n g   *R e a d i n g*

FOCUS ON SKILLS

1. Active Reading

Students are asked to draw pictures of the problem and how it is solved.
Sample Response:

2. Critical Reading Focus

In this lesson, students learn that stories often revolve around one or more problems. The problem and its ultimate solution form the basis of a story's plot. The ability to identify the central problem enables readers to follow the plot and predict what will happen next.

D u r i n g R e a d i n g

FOCUS ON THE SELECTION
Focus on key passages in the selection to make clear how readers can identify the problem and how it is solved in a story.

from "The Wishing Well"
by Arnold Lobel

Ask students, "What do you think the problem will be in this story?"

Page 53

"OUCH!" said the wishing well.

Ask students, "Why do you think the wishing well keeps saying 'OUCH?'"

Page 54

The next day the mouse came back to the well. She threw a penny into the well and made a wish.

"OUCH!" said the well.

"I wish this well would not say ouch," she said.

"OUCH!" said the well. "That hurts!"

Ask students, "How do you think the mouse will solve her problem?"

Ask students, "How could the pillow solve the mouse's problem?"

Page 55

The mouse ran home. She took the pillow from her bed. "This may help," said the mouse, and she ran back to the well.

Have students look at the last picture. Ask them, "What kind of wishes do you think the mouse made?"

Page 56

After that day the mouse made many wishes by the well. And every one of them came true.

After you walk students through these parts of the reading, ask them to consider other ways the mouse might have solved the problem. Ask them, "What could she have done if the pillow had not worked?" Encourage them to share their ideas about other possible solutions. You may even want to draw a simple graphic organizer to show them how they can keep track of the problem and solution in a story.

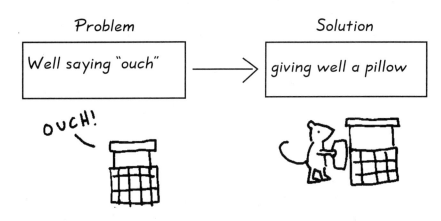

Problem — Well saying "ouch" → Solution — giving well a pillow

After | *Reading*

DISCUSSING THE LITERATURE

Talk about the story with students to help assess their comprehension and understanding of problem-solution structure by asking questions such as:

1. What was the mouse's problem? (*Every time she threw a penny into the wishing well, the wishing well said, "OUCH."*)
2. How did the mouse solve her problem? (*She threw a pillow down the well.*)
3. Do you think you would have liked the story as much if the mouse didn't have a problem to solve? (*Possible: No. The story would be boring.*)

REREADING

After students have read the selection, encourage them to go back and reread any parts that confused them or that they especially enjoyed. Have them share the pictures they drew.

See **Comprehension** on page 142 for more help.

Writing

QUICK ASSESS
Do students' book covers:

✓ show creativity?

✓ illustrate the central problem?

✓ use proper capitalization?

In this lesson, students write about the mouse's problem and how she solved it. Then they make a book cover that illustrates the problem.

WRITING ACTIVITIES

1. The Problem
Students begin to respond to the selection by writing about the mouse's problem.
Sample Response:

> The mouse wanted to make a wish. She threw a penny into the well. The well said "OUCH!"

2. The Solution
Students continue responding to the selection by writing about how the mouse solved her problem.
Sample Response:

The mouse threw a pillow down the wishing well.

3. Making a Book Cover
Students finish responding to the selection by creating a book cover for the story that includes the mouse's problem.
Sample Response:

See **Writing** on page 143 for more help.

WRITING REMINDERS
As students create their covers, remind them to:
• Include the title and author of the story.
• Be creative.
• Be sure to show the mouse's problem.

Vocabulary

WORDS FROM THE SELECTION

Directions: Read each sentence from "The Wishing Well."

Then tell what the underlined word means.

1. "'Now all of my <u>wishes</u> can come true!' she cried."

I think <u>wishes</u> means _____

2. "'<u>OUCH</u>!' said the wishing well."

I think <u>ouch</u> means _____

3. "The next day the mouse came back to the <u>well</u>."

I think <u>well</u> means _____

WORD STUDY: Suffixes

Directions: You can often make a new word by adding a suffix to the end of a word. Add suffixes and write the new words.

_____

1. wish + ing = _____

2. wish + es = _____

3. smart + er = _____

Comprehension

UNDERSTANDING PROBLEM AND SOLUTION

Directions: In the top picture, tell about the mouse's problem. In the bottom picture, tell how she solved her problem.

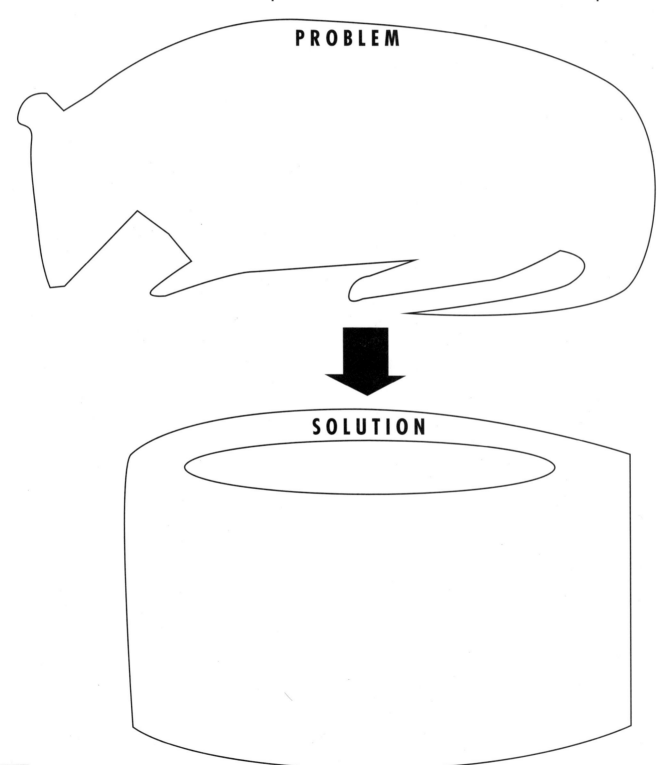

PROBLEM

SOLUTION

Writing

CAPITAL LETTERS

People's names and book titles are capitalized.

Directions: Correct these book covers. Capitalize each writer's name and the titles of the books. Rewrite the book covers with the correct capitalized words.

arnold lobel
"the wishing well"

wade hudson
jamal's busy day

jama kim rattigan
truman's aunt farm

melvin berger
germs make me sick!

Unit Overview

In this unit, students learn about poetry. They explore the way poets use rhyme, choose words to evoke certain feelings in their readers, and paint word pictures. All of these skills enable readers to better understand and appreciate the beauty and meaning of poems. Before starting the unit, talk with students about what they know about poetry. Encourage them to share favorite nursery rhymes and other familiar poems.

Reading the Art

Ask students to look carefully at the art on this page. Then discuss the following questions as a whole-class activity:

- How would you describe this piece of art to a friend?
- Why do you think the word *giggle* is included in the image?
- How does the art make you feel? Why?

Literature Focus

Lesson	Literature
1. Time . . . Dime . . . Rhyme!	**Mary Ann Hoberman,** "Changing"
	The narrator of this poem describes her wish to change places with a friend for a week or so.
2. This Poem Makes Me Feel . . .	**Walter Dean Myers,** "Jeannie Had a Giggle"
	This delightful poem vividly describes Jeannie's giggle as it moves from her toes up to her mouth.
3. Word Pictures	**Nikki Grimes,** "Big Plans"
	The poem describes a girl's big plans for the summer, including eating raspberry ices and walking on the beach.

Reading Focus

Lesson	Reading Skill
1. Time . . . Dime . . . Rhyme!	Note that some sounds in a poem rhyme, or sound the same.
2. This Poem Makes Me Feel . . .	When you read poems, think about how the words make you feel.
3. Word Pictures	When you read poetry, picture the words in your mind.

Writing Focus

Lesson	Writing Assignment
1. Time . . . Dime . . . Rhyme!	Write rhymes for four words.
2. This Poem Makes Me Feel . . .	Finish a poem about the sun, using words that show feelings.
3. Word Pictures	Write a poem about your favorite season.

Time...Dime...Rhyme!

Before *Reading*

FOCUS

Note that some sounds in a poem rhyme, or sound the same.

In this lesson, students learn about the use of rhyme in poetry.

BUILDING BACKGROUND

1. Vocabulary

> know   change   think   wish   could

This relatively simple poem has few challenging words. Rather than use a traditional vocabulary activity, you might instead focus the activity on words that rhyme using this **Rhyme String** activity. Ask one student to think up a rhyming word for *know*. Then ask another student to do the same. See how long students can keep the string of rhymes going. Do the same for the remaining words. Talk about which word had the most rhymes and which had the fewest.

See **Vocabulary** on page 149 for more practice with these words.

2. Prereading

To help students prepare to read this poem, try this **Think-Pair-and-Share** activity. Ask students to explain what clues they can find in each line from the poem that tell them what the poem will be about.
1. "I'd like to change places"
2. "I know what *I* feel like;"
3. "And think what you're thinking"
4. "And you could try me."

ADDITIONAL READING

Additional poems for exploring rhyme include:
My Song Is Beautiful: Poems and Pictures in Many Voices by Mary Ann Hoberman (Little, Brown and Company, 1994)
The Llama Who Had No Pajama by Mary Ann Hoberman (Harcourt Brace, 1998)
Honey, I Love and Other Love Poems by Eloise Greenfield (HarperCollins, 1986)

During *Reading*

FOCUS ON SKILLS

1. Active Reading

Students are asked to circle words in the poem that rhyme.
Sample Response:
week, speak

2. Critical Reading Focus

In this lesson, students learn about the role rhyme plays in poetry. While not all poems rhyme, most poems written for elementary students do. Understanding what rhyme is and why poets use it in their work enables readers to better appreciate poetry and also helps them as they write poetry of their own.

D u r i n g | *R e a d i n g*

FOCUS ON THE SELECTION
Focus on key passages in the poem to make clear what rhyme is and how it can make poems more fun to read.

"Changing"
by Mary Ann Hoberman

Point out the rhyme in this section. Ask students, "How does the beginning of the poem make you feel? Why?"

Page 60

I know what *I* feel like;
I'd like to be you
And feel what *you* feel like
And do what *you* do.

Ask students, "What do you think 'look-like' means?" Point out that besides rhyme, poets can use other forms of word play, such as making up new words, to add fun to their poetry.

Page 61

I'd like to change places
For maybe a week
And look like your look-like
And speak as you speak

Ask students, "What rhyming words did you like the most? Why?"

I wish we could do it;
What fun it would be
If I could try you out
And you could try me.

After you walk students through these parts of the reading, have them work in pairs to read the poem aloud. Point out that poetry is often more fun to read (and listen to) when read aloud.

Encourage them to think about what the poem would be like if the poet had not used any rhyme at all. For instance, read this unrhymed version of the last four lines and ask volunteers to share their reactions:

"I wish we could do it;
What fun it would be
If I could try to be you
And you could imagine my life."

A f t e r   R e a d i n g

DISCUSSING THE LITERATURE
Talk about the poem with students to help assess their comprehension and understanding of rhyme by asking questions such as:
1. Why do you think the poem is called "Changing"? (*Possible: The poem is about changing places with a friend.*)
2. Do you think you would have liked the poem as much if it didn't use rhyme? Why or why not? (*Possible: I would not like it as much because the rhyming words make it fun to read.*)
3. Look back over the poem. What are your favorite lines? (*Possible: "What fun it would be, / If I could try you out, / And you could try me."*)

REREADING
After students have read the poem once, ask one or two volunteers to reread it out loud. Discuss which particular words stand out.

See **Comprehension** on page 150 for more help.

W r i t i n g

QUICK ASSESS
Do students' responses:

✔ demonstrate an understanding of rhyme?

✔ choose real words?

✔ use correct spelling?

In this lesson, students first write some of the rhyming words from the poem and then come up with their own rhyming words.

WRITING ACTIVITIES

1. Finding Rhyming Words
Students begin to respond to the poem by writing three of the rhyming pairs in the poem.
Sample Response:

You rhymes with do.
Speak rhymes with week.
Be rhymes with me.

2. Writing Rhyming Words
Students continue responding to the poem by writing a word that rhymes with the words listed on the page.
Sample Response:

Free rhymes with tree.
Weak rhymes with leak.
Snow rhymes with blow.
Day rhymes with tray.

See **Writing** on page 151 for more help.

WRITING REMINDERS
As students write their rhymes, remind them to:
- Be sure to spell their words correctly.
- Say their word pairs aloud to be sure they rhyme.

Vocabulary

WORDS FROM THE SELECTION

Directions: Read each line from "Changing." Write 1 word that rhymes with the underlined word.

1. "And know what you <u>know</u>."

Know rhymes with _____.

2. "And <u>think</u> what you're thinking"

Think rhymes with _____.

3. "And you <u>could</u> try me."

Could rhymes with _____.

WORD STUDY: Making New Words

Directions: Use the consonants in the box to make new words. An example has been done for you.

l	m	b	s

Old Word	New Word
1. like	bike
2. feet	
3. fun	
4. bake	

Name _____

Comprehension

FINDING RHYME

Directions: Read this poem. Circle the words that rhyme.

"Wishes"

Once I had a special wish.
I asked my mom for a coin
From our magical wish-dish.
My mom said
"What do you need?"
I said, "Why do you ask?
I just wanted to do a good deed."

You see, wishes don't have to be
Only for you.
Wishes are even more special
When they are for somebody new.

GIVING YOUR OPINION

Directions: Write what you like best about "Wishes."

_____
_____
_____
_____
_____

Writing

PRONOUNS

A pronoun is a word that takes the place of a noun.

Example: I like David. <u>He</u> is nice. (<u>He</u> is a pronoun.)

Directions: Rewrite each sentence. Use a pronoun from the word box to take the place of the underlined word.

she	they	it

1. When did <u>Jose and Mattie</u> go for a walk?

_____

- -

_____

2. I really liked <u>this poem</u>.

_____

- -

_____

3. Does <u>my sister</u> want to play soccer?

_____

- -

_____

WRITING

Directions: Pick one of the pronouns from the word box.
How many words can you think of that rhyme with it?
Write those words on the line.

_____

- -

_____

This Poem Makes Me Feel . . .

B e f o r e   R e a d i n g

FOCUS

When you read poems, think about how the words make you feel.

In this lesson, students learn about how poets use words to evoke certain feelings in their readers.

BUILDING BACKGROUND

1. Vocabulary

To help students with the poem's vocabulary, ask them to complete these **Cloze Sentences**. To begin, ask a student to read a sentence with the correct vocabulary word added. Then have students make up new sentences using these words for other students to complete.

> giggle   wiggle   shimmied   slipped   rose

1. I like to *(wiggle)* my loose tooth with my tongue.
2. My dad *(slipped)* on a banana peel and hurt his foot.
3. I *(rose)* from my seat at the end of the movie.
4. The cat *(shimmied)* up the tree.
5. The silly poem made her *(giggle)*.

See **Vocabulary** on page 155 for more practice with these words.

2. Prereading

Give students additional introduction to the poem by **Previewing** it as a whole class. Read the title and first stanza aloud. Have students look at the illustration. Then talk about the preview by discussing questions such as:

1. Who is the poem about? (*a girl named Jeannie*)
2. What do you learn from the title and first few lines of the poem? (*Possible: A girl named Jeannie has a giggle.*)
3. What do you think the rest of the poem will be about? (*Possible: I think the poem will be about how the giggle makes Jeannie feel.*)

ADDITIONAL READING

Additional poems for exploring word play include:
Brown Angels: An Album of Pictures and Verse by Walter Dean Myers (HarperCollins, 1993)
Laugh-eteria by Douglas Florian (Harcourt Brace, 1999)
Small Talk: A Book of Short Poems selected by Lee Bennett Hopkins (Harcourt Brace, 1995)

D u r i n g   R e a d i n g

FOCUS ON SKILLS

1. Active Reading

Students are asked to write how the words in the poem make them feel.
Sample Response:
This makes me feel like giggling.

2. Critical Reading Focus

Poetry can be intimidating for some students. Exposing students at the earliest grades to the sheer joy that poems can provide will help reduce this intimidation. Use this lesson to make clear the fun poets can have with words and the enjoyment readers can get by examining word play in poems.

D u r i n g | *R e a d i n g*

FOCUS ON THE SELECTION
Focus on key passages in the poem to help students see how a poet's choice of words can affect how readers feel as they read.

"Jeannie Had a Giggle"
by Walter Dean Myers

Ask students, "What do you think of the idea of trying to grab a giggle?"

Page 63

She tried to grab the giggle as it
    shimmied past her knees
But it slid right past her fingers with
    a "'scuse me if you please"

Ask students, "Do you like the idea of a giggle flying and jumping? What are your favorite words so far?"

Page 64

Jeannie closed her mouth, but then she heard a funny
    sound
As out that silly giggle flew and jumped down to the
    ground

Ask students, "How do you think you can catch something with this part of your foot?"

Jeannie caught it with her foot just beneath her toes
She gave a little wiggle and up her leg it rose

As you walk students through these parts of the reading, help them focus on particular words. Encourage students to think about how a specific word makes them feel. Have them brainstorm other words the poet might have used in particular lines and think about how these words would affect the poem's meaning or their reactions to it. For instance, read them this alternative ending:

"Jeannie started to laugh once more"

Ask students if they prefer the poem's real last lines. Encourage them to talk specifically about the reasons behind their opinions.

A f t e r   *R e a d i n g*

DISCUSSING THE LITERATURE
Talk about the poem with students to help assess their comprehension and understanding of how poems can make them feel by asking questions such as:
1. "Jeannie Had a Giggle" makes most readers feel happy or silly. How do the words Walter Dean Myers uses help readers feel good? (*Possible: He makes the giggle seem like it is really moving up Jeannie's body.*)
2. What would you tell a friend about this poem? (*Possible: I would tell her to read it because it makes people laugh and smile.*)
3. What words might a poet use to make his or her poem sound scary? (*Possible: Boo!, dark night, spooky*)

REREADING
Have students reread the poem to look for more words or lines that they enjoy. Come together as a class and discuss the reasons for students' choices.

See **Comprehension** on page 156 for more help.

W r i t i n g

QUICK ASSESS
Do students' poems:

✔ describe the sun?

✔ demonstrate an understanding of how words can make readers feel?

✔ show creativity?

In this lesson, students first list their favorite words from the poem. Then they finish a poem about the sun.

WRITING ACTIVITIES

1. Favorite Words
Students begin to respond to the poem by listing two or three favorite words.
Sample Response:
wiggle, flew, shimmied

2. Finishing a Poem
Students continue responding to the poem by finishing a poem about the sun, using words to express feelings.
Sample Response:
The sun is round
and looks so bright.
It glows and sparkles
and makes me feel warm.

See **Writing** on page 157 for more help.

WRITING REMINDERS
As students write their poems, remind them to:
• Use words that show their feelings.
• Be sure the words they choose make sense.
• Read back over their writing to check their spelling.

Vocabulary

WORDS FROM THE SELECTION

Directions: Draw a line from the sentence in Column A to the correct meaning in Column B.

Column A

1. "Jeannie wanted that <u>giggle</u> in"

2. "She tried to grab the giggle as it <u>shimmied</u> past her knees"

3. "She gave a little <u>wiggle</u>"

Column B

silly laugh

move from side to side

shook

WORD STUDY: Prefixes

You can sometimes make a new word by adding a prefix.

re- + view = review

Directions: Add prefixes to the words to make new words.

New Word

1. in- + correct

2. pre- + view

3. dis- + agree

4. un- + safe

Comprehension

DESCRIBING YOUR FEELINGS

Directions: Read the sentence starters below. Finish each sentence. Use words that tell how you feel.

1. Jeannie's giggle makes me feel _____

because_____

_____.

2. Words like *shimmied* and *wiggle* make me feel _____

_____ because _____.

3. I liked this poem because _____

_____.

4. The poem about the moon on page 64 makes me feel

_____ because _____

_____

_____.

Writing

ADJECTIVES

Adjectives are words that tell about people, places, and things.

Example: She gave a <u>little</u> wiggle.

(<u>Little</u> tells us more about the size of the wiggle.)

Directions: Add adjectives to complete these sentences.

1. Yesterday I watched a _____ movie.

2. The star of the movie had _____ hair.

3. I am very _____.

WRITING

Directions: Look at the adjectives in the word box.

How many can you use in 1 sentence?

Write the sentence below.

| little | silly | funny | loud | happy | red |

_____

_____

_____

_____

3 Word Pictures

Before Reading

FOCUS

When you read poetry, picture the words in your mind.

In this lesson, students learn how poets use words to help readers visualize their ideas.

BUILDING BACKGROUND

1. Vocabulary

To help familiarize students with the poem's vocabulary, have them complete this **Vocabulary Inventory**. Have students write the following words on a piece of paper:

surrender   ices   barbecue   lick   spoil

Then have students place a mark next to each word to indicate how well they know it (+ = know this word, ? = seems familiar, 0 = don't know this word). After students complete the inventory, come together as a class and discuss their markings. Encourage students to make predictions about what the poem will be about based on these key vocabulary words.

See **Vocabulary** on page 161 for more practice with these words.

2. Prereading

Give students additional introduction to the poem by creating a **Word Web** around the word *summer*. Discuss the questions with students.

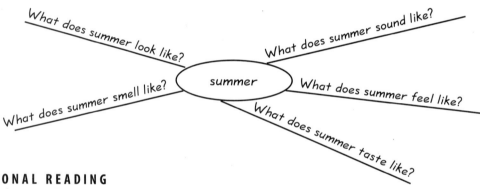

What does summer look like?
What does summer smell like?
summer
What does summer sound like?
What does summer feel like?
What does summer taste like?

ADDITIONAL READING

Additional poems for exploring visualization include:
Touch the Poem by Arnold Adoff (Blue Sky Press, 2000)
Lunch Money and Other Poems About School by Carol Diggory Shields (Dutton Books, 1995)
All the Colors of the Earth by Sheila Hamanaka (William Morrow and Company, 1994)

During Reading

FOCUS ON SKILLS

1. Active Reading

Students are asked to draw things they "see" in the poem.
Sample Response:

2. Critical Reading Focus

The beauty of a poem often lies in its use of imagery. Sensory details help readers imagine what the poet is describing. Details that focus on the five senses enable readers to experience the poem, rather than just read it. Use this lesson to help students see the power of sensory images.

During Reading

FOCUS ON THE SELECTION
Focus on key passages in the poem to help students understand how poets use words to help their readers "see" what they read.

"Big Plans"
by Nikki Grimes

Ask students, "What does it mean to 'surrender to summer'?"

Page 66
surrender
to
summer,

Ask students, "What do you see so far?"

and
walks on the beach

Ask students, "What sights, sounds, and smells would you expect at a zoo?"

Page 67
and
at least
one
trip to the zoo,

Have students close their eyes. Ask them to picture the poem in their mind. Ask students, "What do you see? What would you like to do on a summer afternoon?"

never a lick
of
homework to spoil
one
afternoon.

After you walk students through these parts of the poem, have them look for more "picture words." Come together as a class and discuss students' ideas. You may want to make a list on the board of sights, sounds, and smells that students associate with summer that this poem calls to their minds. Suggest to students that they can use a Web to keep track of words and ideas.

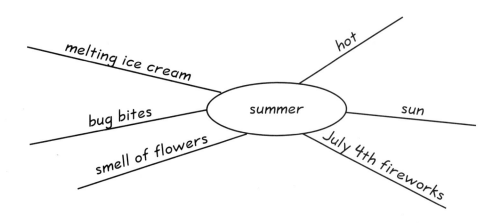

A f t e r   R e a d i n g

DISCUSSING THE LITERATURE

Talk about the poem with students to help assess their comprehension and understanding of how poets use words to help their readers "see" a poem:

1. How do you think Nikki Grimes feels about summer? Why? (*Possible: I can tell she likes it because she talks about all the good things about summer.*)
2. Was it easy or hard to picture Nikki Grimes's ideas in your head as you read the poem? Why? (*Possible: It was easy because she used lots of words that make me think about summer.*)
3. What is your favorite part of the poem? Why? (*Possible: I liked "Never a lick of homework to spoil one afternoon." That's my favorite part of summer!*)

REREADING

After students have finished reading the poem once, encourage them to go back to particular words or lines and talk about the pictures they drew.

See **Comprehension** on page 162 for more help.

W r i t i n g

In this lesson, students first return to the images in the poem. Then they think about their favorite season, draw a picture of it, and finally write a poem about it.

WRITING ACTIVITIES

1. "Picture" Words

Students circle any words they can picture in their minds and then write and draw pictures of three things they can see.
Sample Response:
family barbecue

2. A Favorite Season

Students select their favorite season, list two or three words that describe it, and draw a picture of it.
Sample Response:
spring—cool, flowers

3. Writing a Poem

Students choose words to complete a poem about their favorite season.
Sample Response:
My favorite season is spring.
Because it makes me feel like being outside and seeing flowers.

See **Writing** on page 163 for more help.

WRITING REMINDERS

As students draw their pictures, remind them to:

- Use their words to help them describe the season.
- Be creative.
- Check their spelling.

Vocabulary

WORDS FROM THE SELECTION

Directions: Read each sentence. Use a word from the word box to complete each sentence.

surrender   barbecue   spoil

1. We went to my aunt's house for a _____ last night.

2. The robber would not _____ to the police.

3. The rain will _____ our game.

WORD STUDY: Compound Words

A compound word is a word made up of two smaller words.

afternoon = after + noon

Directions: Break the compound word into two smaller words.

homework = _____ + _____

grandfather = _____ + _____

mailbox = _____ + _____

snowball = _____ + _____

Comprehension

PICTURING A POEM

Directions: Read the words from the poem in the first column. In the second column, draw what you see.

Double-entry Journal

Words from the Poem	What I See
"trip to the zoo"	
"Sunday school picnic"	

GIVING YOUR OPINION

Directions: Tell what you liked best about "Big Plans."

_____

_____

_____

_____

CAPITAL LETTERS AND PERIODS

Directions: Mark an X in front of each sentence that starts with a capital letter and ends with a period.

_____1. Summer begins in June.

_____2. susan loves to go to the beach in the summer.

_____3. I like fall better

_____4. Winter is fun because of the snow.

_____5. spring flowers are so pretty.

WRITING

Directions: Write a sentence telling how you feel about "Big Plans."

Be sure to begin the sentence with a capital letter and end it with a period.

Unit Overview

In this unit, students learn more about nonfiction writing. While Unit Two focused on the importance of understanding the main idea and details of a nonfiction piece, this unit expands on students' understanding. Here students explore how to keep track of the order of events, how graphic organizers can help organize their thinking, and how retelling helps them better understand and remember important information.

Reading the Art

Ask students to look carefully at the art on this page. Then discuss the following questions as a whole-class activity:

- How would you describe this piece of art to a friend?
- What clues does the art give you about what the unit might be about?
- How does the image of the elephant make you feel? Why?

L i t e r a t u r e   F o c u s

Lesson	Literature
1. What Does It Mean?	**Paula Z. Hogan,** from *The Elephant*
	Readers discover fascinating facts about elephants in this informative nonfiction piece.
2. Know What Happens	**Sabrina Crewe,** from *The Alligator*
	Readers learn about the life of baby alligators in this engaging selection.
3. Read to Understand	**Kimberly Brubaker Bradley,** from *Pop! A Book About Bubbles*
	Readers explore bubbles, from what they are made of to how to blow them.

R e a d i n g   F o c u s

Lesson	Reading Skill
1. What Does It Mean?	As you read, ask, "What is this all about?"
2. Know What Happens	Look for the order of things as you read.
3. Read to Understand	Make a Web to understand what you read.

W r i t i n g   F o c u s

Lesson	Writing Assignment
1. What Does It Mean?	Create a sign about elephants at the zoo.
2. Know What Happens	Write the order of things in an alligator's life.
3. Read to Understand	Explain to a friend how to blow bubbles.

1   What Does It Mean?

Before Reading

FOCUS

As you read, ask, "What is this all about?"

In this lesson, students learn how to keep track of important ideas in nonfiction writing.

BUILDING BACKGROUND

1. Vocabulary

several   herd   female   tusks   adults

Try a **Vocabulary Quiz Show** to help students learn the above vocabulary words. Write each word on a 3 x 5 card. Then write a definition for each word on five other cards. Distribute the cards to different students in class. Begin by asking one student to say one of the words. Then have the students holding the card with the meaning of the word read that card aloud. Continue until you are satisfied that all students are familiar with the words.

See **Vocabulary** on page 169 for more practice with these words.

2. Prereading

Use an **Anticipation Guide** to build more background for the selection.

1. Agree   Disagree   Elephants live by themselves.
2. Agree   Disagree   Elephants are the largest animals on land.
3. Agree   Disagree   Elephants are born with tusks.
4. Agree   Disagree   Elephants are mean and fight a lot.

ADDITIONAL READING

Additional nonfiction books for exploring animals include:
All About Turkeys by Jim Arnosky (Scholastic, 1998)
Prairie Dogs by Emery Bernhard (Harcourt Brace, 1997)
As the Roadrunner Runs by Gail Hartman (Bradbury, 1994)

During Reading

FOCUS ON SKILLS

1. Active Reading

Students are asked to underline important ideas in the selection.
Sample Response:
"They are the largest animals on land."

2. Critical Reading Focus

Informational text teaches readers about a topic. Writers have the responsibility of providing facts about the topic; readers have the responsibility of asking questions as they read to help them determine what the writer is trying to teach them. Use this lesson to sharpen students' ability to identify essential information in informational texts. Stress how important it is for students to keep thinking of what the writer is trying to get across in each paragraph or on each page.

During | *Reading*

FOCUS ON THE SELECTION
Focus on key passages in the selection to help students understand how to identify important information in nonfiction texts.

from *The Elephant*
by Paula Z. Hogan

Ask students, "What is the writer trying to teach you in this paragraph?"

Page 72

A newborn elephant tries to walk right after birth. At first it trips and falls. Two days later a baby can keep up with the adults.

Ask students, "What is the most surprising fact you have learned so far?"

Page 73

Several elephants live in a herd. All the adults help care for the baby. An older female leads the herd.

Ask students, "What is the most important fact in this paragraph? Why?"

Elephants are very friendly. They greet each other by touching with their trunks. Herds sometimes join together.

Ask students, "What do you learn in this paragraph?"

Page 74

Young elephants must learn to drink with their trunks. They suck up water and pour it into their mouths.

Ask students, "What is this paragraph about?"

When they are about two years old, young elephants begin to grow tusks. They can use tusks to push down trees. That's how elephants eat leaves from the highest branches.

As you review specific passages from the reading, be sure students recognize that each paragraph focuses on a different topic about elephants: how they walk, what they eat, how they drink, and so on. Ask students to find the most important idea in selected paragraphs from the selection. Invite students to work in pairs to share their ideas.

A f t e r   *R e a d i n g*

DISCUSSING THE LITERATURE

Talk about the selection with students to help assess their comprehension and understanding of nonfiction writing:

1. What was the most interesting fact you learned about elephants? (*Possible: Elephants are very friendly.*)
2. What do you think the writer was trying to teach you about elephants? (*Possible: She wanted to tell me about how elephants live.*)
3. How did you decide what ideas to underline? (*Possible: I looked for the most important facts.*)

REREADING

After students finish reading the selection, encourage them to review what they underlined. Suggest that they reread and, as they do, underline additional important information.

See **Comprehension** on page 170 for more help.

W r i t i n g

QUICK ASSESS

Do students' signs:

✓ include details from the selection?

✓ demonstrate what students learned from the selection?

✓ show creativity?

In this lesson, students first list a few important ideas from the selection. Then they read a series of facts and mark those that are true. Finally, they use their notes to write a sign about elephants.

WRITING ACTIVITIES

1. The Facts

Students begin to respond to the selection by listing two or three important facts they learned about elephants.
Sample Response:

A baby elephant is heavier than a man, and it is very friendly.

2. The Details

Students continue responding to the selection by reading a list of facts about elephants and marking those that are true.
Sample Response:

X's next to all but two—the third and last detail

3. Creating a Sign

Students continue responding to the selection by using the details they marked to create a sign for elephants at the zoo.
Sample Response:

Elephants are friendly. They are the largest land animals. Watch them use their trunks to drink.

See **Writing** on page 171 for more help.

WRITING REMINDERS

As students write their signs, remind them to:
- Use details from their notes.
- Check that all words are spelled correctly.
- Use correct punctuation.

Vocabulary

WORDS FROM THE SELECTION

Directions: Write a word from the box to fill in each sentence.

several female adults

1. Usually, _____ elephants live together.

2. All the _____ take care of the baby elephants.

3. An older _____ elephant is in charge of all the others.

WORD STUDY: Prefixes and Suffixes

Directions: Add a prefix or suffix to each of the small words to make a new word.

Bigger Word

1. un- + happy = _____

2. re- + read = _____

3. smell + -ing = _____

4. call + -ed = _____

Comprehension

TELLING WHAT YOU LEARNED

Directions: Tell what you learned about elephants from reading *The Elephant.*

What I Know About:

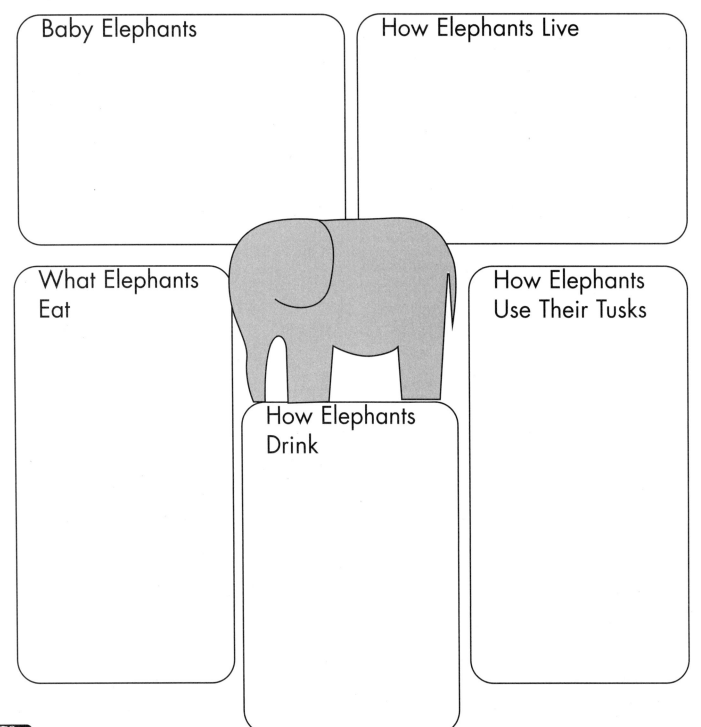

Baby Elephants

How Elephants Live

What Elephants Eat

How Elephants Use Their Tusks

How Elephants Drink

Writing

QUESTIONS AND EXCLAMATIONS

An asking sentence asks a question and ends with a question mark.

Where do elephants live?

An exclamatory sentence shows strong feelings and ends with an exclamation point.

I love elephants!

Directions: Write a ? (question mark) or ! (exclamation point) to finish each sentence.

What do elephants eat

Elephants are amazing

Why do elephants have tusks

You're terrific

Who told you about this book

WRITING

Write a question about elephants.

_____

- -

_____

- -

_____

- -

_____

Know What Happens

B e f o r e   R e a d i n g

FOCUS
Look for the order of things as you read.

In this lesson, students learn how to keep track of the sequence of events in nonfiction writing.

BUILDING BACKGROUND

1. Vocabulary

twigs   predators   scoop   snout   hatch

Before reading the selection, make sure students understand the above vocabulary words. Use a **Context Clues** activity to help them. Work with students to figure out the meaning of the underlined word in each sentence.

1. "The mother alligator <u>scoops</u> the babies into her large mouth."
2. "Baby alligators use a special tooth on their <u>snouts</u> to cut through the tough layer."
3. "Baby alligators can swim from the moment they <u>hatch</u>."
4. "Now she will cover the eggs with leaves and <u>twigs</u>."
5. "She will stop any <u>predators</u> from taking her eggs."

See **Vocabulary** on page 175 for more practice with these words.

2. Prereading

Provide additional introduction to the selection by **Previewing** it as a whole class. Read the title and first paragraph aloud. Have students look at the illustrations. Then talk about the preview by discussing questions such as:

1. What is the selection about? (*alligators*)
2. What do you already know about alligators? (*Possible: I know they lay eggs.*)
3. What do you hope to learn about alligators from reading this selection? (*Possible: I want to know how they take care of their babies.*)

ADDITIONAL READING
Additional nonfiction by Sabrina Crewe includes:
The Kangaroo (Raintree Steck-Vaughn, 1997)
The Ladybug (Raintree Steck-Vaughn, 1997)
The Bee (Raintree Steck-Vaughn, 1997)

D u r i n g   R e a d i n g

FOCUS ON SKILLS

1. Active Reading
Students are asked to write two or three things that happen on each page of the selection.
Sample Response:
She lays eggs and watches over the nest.

2. Critical Reading Focus
Often informational text is written in sequential order. Understanding the sequence of events in such writing is critical to understanding the selection and remembering essential information. Use this lesson to help students begin to understand the text structure underlying this type of nonfiction by pointing out clue words, such as *next*, *then*, and *now*.

D u r i n g | *R e a d i n g*

FOCUS ON THE SELECTION
Focus on key passages in the selection to help students understand how to use key words to follow the sequence of events in a nonfiction selection.

from ***The Alligator***
by Sabrina Crewe

Page 77

Point out that one way to keep track of the order of how things happen in a selection is to look for clue words such as *now*, *then*, and *next*. Ask students, "What clue word do you find here?"

It is summer. The alligator has laid her eggs in a hole on top of her nest. Now she will cover the eggs with leaves and twigs. Inside the eggs, baby alligators are growing.

Page 78

Point out the clue words *after* and *then* in this paragraph. Ask students to retell what happens in the paragraph using the clue words as guides.

The baby alligators come out of their eggs. After about two months, the hard shell of the egg starts to crack. Under the hard shell is another, tough layer. Baby alligators use a special tooth on their snouts to cut through the tough layer. Then they hatch from their eggs.

Page 79

Ask students, "What do you learn about alligators here? Do you recognize any clue words?"

The mother alligator carries her babies. The mother alligator scoops the babies into her large mouth. She takes them from the nest to the edge of the pool. Then she drops them in the water. The mother makes several trips to get all the babies to the pool.

After you walk students through these parts of the reading, ask them to return to the selection to look for more clue words that tell them what happens first, second, and so forth. Brainstorm a list of additional clue words (*first, next, later, at the same time, last,* and so on). Have students point out sentences in the selection where they could add some of these key words.

You might also suggest that students list some things that happen in a simple Sequence Chart.

A f t e r   R e a d i n g

DISCUSSING THE LITERATURE
Talk about the selection with students to help assess their comprehension of the selection and understanding of sequence by asking questions such as:
1. What are some clue words that the writer uses to help you keep track of what happens? (*Possible: now, then, and after*)
2. How can the clue words help you keep track of what happens? (*Possible: They let me know what happens when.*)
3. How did you decide what ideas to make notes about? (*Possible: I looked for the most important facts about alligators.*)

REREADING
After students finish reading the selection, suggest that they share what they wrote with a partner. Encourage them to reread parts of the piece that they might not have understood or remembered.

See **Comprehension** on page 176 for more help.

W r i t i n g

QUICK ASSESS
Do students' notes:

✔ demonstrate an understanding of the life cycle of baby alligators?

✔ tell what happens in the correct order?

✔ use complete sentences?

In this lesson, students fill in a chart that lists four things that happen in an alligator's life.

WRITING ACTIVITIES

1. What Happens First
Students begin to respond to the selection by using their notes to tell what happens first in the selection.
Sample Response:
The mama alligator lays her eggs. She watches over them.

2. What Happens Second
Students continue responding to the selection by writing what happens next.
Sample Response:
The baby alligators hatch. They are very small.

3. What Happens Next
Students continue responding to the selection by writing what happens next.
Sample Response:
The baby alligators call for their mom. Their mom takes them out of the nest.

See **Writing** on page 177 for more help.

WRITING REMINDERS
As students write what happens in the selection, remind them to:
- Use their notes and clue words to help them keep track of what happens when.
- Use complete sentences.
- Check to see that each sentence begins with a capital letter and ends with a period, question mark, or exclamation point.

Vocabulary

WORDS FROM THE SELECTION

Directions: Use words from the box to fill in each sentence.

scoop   snout   hatch

1. Baby alligators _____ from eggs.

2. An alligator's long front part is called a _____.

3. Mother alligators _____ their babies out of the nest.

WORD STUDY: Contractions

You put together two small words to make a contraction. Use an apostrophe to take the place of the letter or letters you leave out.

I am = I'm

Directions: Write the contraction form for each of the following.

<u>Two Words</u>	<u>Contraction</u>
1. it is	
2. did not	
3. she is	
4. let us	

Comprehension

UNDERSTANDING THE ORDER OF EVENTS

Directions: Retell 4 events in an alligator's life. Draw pictures of what happens.

1.

2.

3.

4.

Writing

COMPLETE SENTENCES

Directions: Mark an X in front of each complete sentence.

_____1. Baby alligators call for their mom.

_____2. Hatching from eggs.

_____3. Swim in the water.

_____4. Alligators lay eggs.

_____5. A nest of leaves and twigs.

WRITING

Directions: Write a complete sentence about alligators to show what you learned from this selection.

_____

_____

_____

_____

_____

_____

_____

3 Read to Understand

B e f o r e   R e a d i n g

FOCUS

Make a web to help you understand what you read.

In this lesson, students learn how to identify the topic of a piece of writing.

BUILDING BACKGROUND

1. Vocabulary

To help familiarize students with the selection's vocabulary, have them complete this **Vocabulary Inventory**. Have students write the following words on a piece of paper:

   plastic   float   shimmers   liquid   snaps

Then have students place a mark next to each word to indicate how well they know it (+ = know this word, ? = seems familiar, 0 = don't know this word). After students complete the inventory, come together as a class and discuss their markings. Encourage students to make predictions about what the selection will be about based on these key vocabulary words.

See **Vocabulary** on page 181 for more practice with these words.

2. Prereading

Try this **Think-Pair-and-Share** activity to activate students' prior knowledge about bubbles. Ask students to read these sentences and then answer the questions.
1. "Finally it snaps free."
2. "When you blow into the wand, you make air move."
3. "Dip the plastic wand into the soap solution."
4. "As you blow harder, the soap stretches and stretches until it can't stretch anymore."

Questions:
1. Which sentence tells you what happens at the end of blowing a bubble? (*sentence number 1*)
2. Which sentence tells you what to do first when you blow a bubble? (*sentence number 3*)
3. Which two sentences tells you what happens in between? (*sentences 2 and 4*)

ADDITIONAL READING

Additional nonfiction for exploring a topic and details about the topic include:
Throw Your Tooth on the Roof: Tooth Traditions from Around the World by Selby B. Beeler
    (Houghton Mifflin, 1998)
Biggest, Strongest, Fastest by Steve Jenkins (Ticknor and Fields, 1995)
The Popcorn Book by Tomie dePaola (Holiday House, 1978)

D u r i n g   R e a d i n g

FOCUS ON SKILLS

1. Active Reading

Students are asked to underline important details on each page of the selection.
Sample Response:
"Hold it up to your mouth."

2. Critical Reading Focus

In early lessons, students explored main idea and details. Use this lesson to explore a broader category—the topic of a piece of informational text. Help students see the value of using graphic organizers to help them understand and retain information about the topic of a piece of nonfiction.

During Reading

FOCUS ON THE SELECTION

Focus on key passages in the selection to help students understand how to identify the selection's topic and important details.

From *Pop! A Book About Bubbles*
by Kimberly Brubaker Bradley

Point out that this first page of the selection lets the reader know what the topic is—bubbles. Be sure students notice the clue to the topic in the title. Explain that the main, or big idea, of the selection is how to blow bubbles. Talk about the differences between the topic and the main idea.

Page 82

Phhhh! You've made a bubble.

Watch it float higher and higher.

The bubble shimmers in the sun.

You can blow small bubbles or big ones.

Ask students, "What do you learn about bubbles here?"

Page 83

Bubbles are air trapped inside liquid.

It is sticky. It sticks to the floor if you spill it. It sticks to your fingers when you touch it. And it sticks to the plastic bubble wand. It sticks and it stretches. It stretches across the round hole on the end of the bubble wand.

Point out how the writer repeats, "It sticks …" over and over again in this paragraph. Ask students, "Why do you think the writer does this?"

Page 84

Finally it snaps free. The soap shuts around the air inside it. There it is!
A bubble!

Remind students what they learned about writers telling things in the order they happen. Point out that Kimberly Brubaker Bradley does this in this part of the section.

After you walk students through these parts of the reading, discuss together where they can look for clues about the topic of a selection. Tell them that clues are often in the title, the first and last paragraphs, and in repeated words.

A f t e r   R e a d i n g

DISCUSSING THE LITERATURE

Talk with students to help assess their comprehension of the selection by asking questions such as:

1. What is this selection all about? (*how to make bubbles*)
2. What are three important details you learned from this selection? (*Possible: Bubbles cannot be square. Bubbles are made from soap and water. All bubbles are round.*)
3. What is the most surprising fact you learned about bubbles in this section? (*Possible: I did not know that you couldn't make square bubbles.*)

REREADING

After students have finished reading the selection, suggest that they review what they underlined as they reread. Encourage them to look for additional details.

See **Comprehension** on page 182 for more help.

W r i t i n g

QUICK ASSESS

Do students' explanations:

✔ demonstrate an understanding of how bubbles are formed?

✔ tell what happens in the correct order?

✔ include information from their Web?

In this lesson, students fill in a Web about how to make bubbles and then use their notes to tell a friend how to blow bubbles.

WRITING ACTIVITIES

1. Making a Web

Students begin to respond to the selection by completing a Web that shows the three steps for making a bubble.

Sample Response:

1. Dip your bubble wand into the bubble solution.
2. Blow into the wand.
3. Keep blowing until the bubble breaks free from the wand and floats away.

2. Explaining How to Blow Bubbles

Students continue responding to the selection by using their notes to explain to a friend how to blow bubbles.

Sample Response:

First, you need a plastic wand and bubble solution. You can make your own bubble solution with soap and water. Next, you put your wand in the bubble mixture. Then you blow gently into the wand. Keep blowing until the bubble breaks away from the wand. Watch the bubble float away.

See **Writing** on page 183 for more help.

WRITING REMINDERS

As students write their explanations, remind them to:

- Be sure to tell the steps in the correct order.
- Use complete sentences.
- Check to see that each word is spelled correctly.

Vocabulary

WORDS FROM THE SELECTION

Directions: Read each sentence. Tell what you think the underlined words mean.

plastic float shimmers liquid snaps

1. "Watch it <u>float</u> higher and higher."

I think <u>float</u> means _____.

2. "The bubble <u>shimmers</u> in the sun."

I think <u>shimmer</u> means _____.

3. "Dip the <u>plastic</u> wand into the soap solution"

I think <u>plastic</u> means _____.

4. "Bubbles are trapped inside <u>liquid</u>."

I think <u>liquid</u> means _____.

5. "Finally it <u>snaps</u> free."

I think <u>snap</u> means _____.

Comprehension

CHECKING UNDERSTANDING

Directions: Write the topic of the selection in the first box. Write the main idea (the most important idea about the topic) in the second box and 2 details in the bottom boxes.

Topic

Main Idea

Detail

Detail

Writing

SOUND-ALIKE WORDS

Some words sound alike but have different spellings. They also have different meanings. These words are called *homophones*.

I _blew_ a bubble with a _blue_ plastic wand.

Directions: Circle the correct word to finish each sentence.

1. Ling winked his (eye/I).
2. I want to come (too/two).
3. My baby sister has a teddy (bare/bear).
4. What did you get (for/four) your birthday?
5. Sam (ate/eight) an apple.

WRITING

Directions: Write a sentence using each of these homophones.

1. (to) _____

_____

2. (too) _____

_____

3. (two) _____

_____

U n i t   O v e r v i e w

In this final unit, students explore three more authors: Gary Soto, Simon James, and Jane Yolen. As they read the stories, they expand on their understanding of problem-solution structure, the importance of connecting to their reading, and how to identify an author's message.

R e a d i n g   t h e   A r t

Ask students to look carefully at the art on this page. Then discuss the following questions as a whole-class activity:

- What do you see?
- How would you describe the owl?
- How does this image make you feel? Why?

L i t e r a t u r e   F o c u s

Lesson	Literature
1. What's the Problem?	**Gary Soto,** from *Too Many Tamales*
	Maria gets herself into quite a mess when she loses her mother's ring.
2. What Do I Think?	**Simon James,** from *Dear Mr. Blueberry*
	Through a series of letters, Mr. Blueberry tries to convince Emily that she does not have a whale living in her pond.
3. What's It All Mean?	**Jane Yolen,** from *Owl Moon*
	A girl and her father go owling one night and spot a magnificent owl.

R e a d i n g   F o c u s

Lesson	Reading Skill
1. What's the Problem?	Look for the problem and how it is solved in a story.
2. What Do I Think?	As you read, ask yourself, "What do I think about this story?"
3. What's It All Mean?	As you read, ask yourself, "What is the author trying to say to me?"

W r i t i n g   F o c u s

Lesson	Writing Assignment
1. What's the Problem?	Write about a time you lost something.
2. What Do I Think?	Write a book review of the story.
3. What's It All Mean?	Write a story about an animal.

What's the Problem?

B e f o r e   *R e a d i n g*

FOCUS

Look for the problem and how it is solved in a story.

In this lesson, students expand on their understanding of the role conflict plays in fiction.

BUILDING BACKGROUND

1. Vocabulary

To help familiarize students with the selection's vocabulary, have them complete this **Vocabulary Inventory**. Have students write the following words on a piece of paper:

   tamales   kneaded   husks   drifted   dusk

Then have students place a mark next to each word to indicate how well they know it (+ = know this word, ? = seems familiar, 0 = don't know this word). After students complete the inventory, come together as a class and discuss their markings. Encourage students to make predictions about what the selection will be about based on these key vocabulary words.

See **Vocabulary** on page 189 for more practice with these words.

2. Prereading

Provide additional introduction to the selection by **Previewing** it as a whole class. Read the title and first two paragraphs aloud. Have students look at the illustrations. Then talk about the preview by discussing questions such as:

1. What do you think this story will be about? (*Possible: people celebrating a holiday or something that happens with the tamales*)
2. Who do you think the story will be about? (*a girl named Maria and her family*)
3. What do you learn from the beginning of the story? (*Possible: It is a winter day at dusk. Maria is helping her mom make tamales.*)

ADDITIONAL READING

Additional works by Gary Soto include:

Snapshots from a Wedding (Putnam, 1997)
Chato's Kitchen (Chato Y Su Cena) (Putnam, 1995)

D u r i n g   *R e a d i n g*

FOCUS ON SKILLS

1. Active Reading

Students are asked to pause after reading each page of the story and ask a question about what they think will happen.

Sample Response:

Why are they making tamales?

2. Critical Reading Focus

Conflict is at the heart of a story's plot. Without a problem to overcome, the plot of a story would be rather dull. Use this lesson to help students better understand and appreciate how characters' problems make a reading more interesting.

During Reading

FOCUS ON THE SELECTION
Focus on key passages in the selection to help students understand how to identify a character's problem in a story.

from ***Too Many Tamales***
by Gary Soto

Page 88

Their hands were sticky with <u>masa</u>.

Point out that when an unfamiliar word is underlined, as *masa* is, it lets the reader know that a definition of the word can be found at the bottom of the page.

Page 89

She felt grown-up, wearing her mother's apron. Her mom had even let her wear lipstick and perfume. If only I could wear Mom's ring, she thought to herself.

"I'll wear the ring for just a minute," she said to herself. The ring sparkled on her thumb.

Ask students, "What do you learn about Maria here?"

Ask students, "What do you think will happen next? Why?"

Page 90

Maria returned to kneading the *masa*, her hands pumping up and down. On her thumb the ring disappeared, then reappeared in the sticky glob of dough.

Point out how often Gary Soto mentions the ring in the first two pages. Explain that this gives his readers a hint that somehow the ring is going to be part of Maria's problem.

Page 92

"The ring!" she screamed.
Everyone stared at her. "What ring?" Dolores asked.
Without answering, Maria ran to the kitchen.

Ask students, "What's Maria's problem? How do you think she will solve it?"

Page 93

"Eat them," she said. "If you bite something hard, tell me."

Ask students, "Why does Maria ask her cousins to eat the tamales? Do you think they will help her solve her problem?"

As you walk students through these parts of the reading, help them focus on Maria's problem. Encourage them to discuss other ways she might have tried to solve it.

A f t e r   R e a d i n g

DISCUSSING THE LITERATURE
Talk with students to help assess their comprehension of the story by asking questions such as:
1. How would you describe Maria? (*Possible: She is a very helpful girl who wants to be more grown-up.*)
2. Why does Maria put on her mother's ring? (*Possible: She thinks it is beautiful and wants to feel more grown-up.*)
3. What happens after Maria puts on the ring? (*She loses it when she is making tamales. She asks her cousins to eat the tamales to find it.*)

REREADING
After they finish reading the selection, have students review the notes they made. Ask them to reread the selection to look for hints about the story's problem.

See **Comprehension** on page 190 for more help.

W r i t i n g

QUICK ASSESS
Do students' paragraphs:

✔ clearly state their problem and how they solved it?

✔ use the first-person point of view?

✔ use complete sentences?

In this lesson, students fill out a chart about the selection and then write about a time when they lost something.

WRITING ACTIVITIES

1. Problem-Solution Map
Students begin to respond to the selection by completing a Problem-Solution Map.
Sample Response:
Problem: Maria loses her mother's ring when she is making tamales.
Solution: Maria asks her cousins to eat the tamales to find the ring.

2. Writing about a Problem
Students continue responding to the selection by writing about a time when they have lost something and how they found it.
Sample Response:
I lost my dog one day. I forgot to close the door. I started to cry. Then I tried to figure out a way to find my dog. My dad and I went searching for him. I kept calling his name. We started walking home. Guess what? My dog was waiting for us on our front porch!

See **Writing** on page 191 for more help.

WRITING REMINDERS
As students write their paragraphs, remind them to:
- Use first-person pronouns.
- Use complete sentences.
- Be sure they explain both the problem and how they solved it.

Vocabulary

WORDS FROM THE SELECTION

Directions: Draw a line from each word to its meaning.

tamales   the time of day just before the sun goes down

kneaded   moved by the wind

husks   mixed and pressed together with your hands

drifted   a dish made from chopped meat that is rolled in cornmeal

dusk   the dry outside covering of corn

WORD STUDY: Plurals

You can make the plural form of many words by adding an *s*.

boy/boys   book/books   cat/cats

Directions: Read the sentences. Circle all the plural words that end in <u>s</u>. There are 7 plurals in all.

1. The cars cost a lot of money.
2. Where did the dogs hide their bones?
3. The cakes and pies tasted good.
4. Sammy will draw pictures.
5. I have new red shoes.

Comprehension

CHECKING UNDERSTANDING

Directions: Put an X next to each statement that is false.

_____1. Maria wears her mother's apron.

_____2. Maria has fun with her cats and dogs.

_____3. The story takes place in the summer.

_____4. Maria drops her mother's ring down the sink.

_____5. Maria and her mom make a cherry pie.

REWRITING SENTENCES

Directions: Rewrite 2 of the sentences that are false to make them true.

1. _____

_____

_____

2. _____

_____

_____

Writing

WRITING COMPLETE SENTENCES

Directions: Match words from Column A with words from Column B to make complete sentences. Write the complete sentences on the lines.

Column A	Column B
Maria wants	her mother's ring.
Maria plays	her cousins for help.
Maria loses	to be more grown-up.
Maria asks	with her cousins.

1. _____

2. _____

3. _____

4. _____

2 What Do I Think?

Before Reading

FOCUS

As you read, ask yourself, "What do I think about this story?"

In this lesson, students explore ways to connect a story to their own life.

BUILDING BACKGROUND

1. Vocabulary

pond   information   details   sincerely   pleased

Try a **Vocabulary Quiz Show** to help students learn the above vocabulary words. Write each word on a 3 x 5 card. Then write a definition for each word on five other cards. Distribute the cards to different students in class. Begin by asking one student to say one of the words. Then have the student holding the card with the meaning of the word read the card aloud. Continue until you are satisfied that all students are familiar with the words.

See **Vocabulary** on page 195 for more practice with these words.

2. Prereading

To help activate students' prior knowledge, create a **Word Web** around the word *whales*.

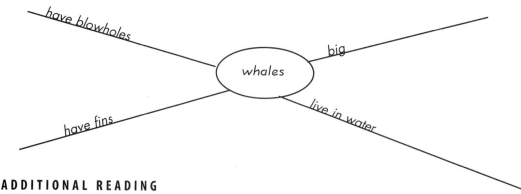

have blowholes

big

whales

have fins

live in water

ADDITIONAL READING

Additional works by Simon James include:
Leon and Bob (Candlewick Press, 1997)
The Wild Woods (Candlewick Press, 1993)
Sally and the Limpet (M. K. McElderry Books, 1990)

During Reading

FOCUS ON SKILLS

1. Active Reading

Students are asked to write how the story is like something in their lives.
Sample Response:
I like whales, too.

2. Critical Reading Focus

Connecting to the text is one way readers can get more actively involved in the material. By making connections between what is happening in a story and their own lives, readers become much more engaged in the reading process. Use this lesson to help students recognize how connecting to the text can help them better understand and enjoy their reading.

D u r i n g   R e a d i n g

FOCUS ON THE SELECTION
Focus on key passages in the story to help students understand how to connect to the text and decide what they think of a story.

from *Dear Mr. Blueberry*
by Simon James

As students begin to read, make sure they understand that Mr. Blueberry is Emily's teacher. Ask students, "What do you think of this story so far? Why?"

Page 96

Dear Emily,

Here are some details about whales. I don't think you'll find it was a whale you saw, because whales don't live in ponds, but in salt water.

Yours sincerely
Your teacher,
Mr. Blueberry

Ask students, "How is this story like something you know?" Help students connect to times when they've been worried about an animal.

Page 97

Do you think he might be lost?

Love, Emily

Ask students, "What else do you know about whales or oceans?"

I'm afraid there can't be a whale in your pond, because whales don't get lost, they always know where they are in the oceans.

Yours sincerely,
Mr. Blueberry

As you walk students through parts of the reading, encourage them to relate the story to their own lives by sharing some of the connections you can make. For instance, perhaps you have seen a whale, lived near a saltwater ocean, or once written a letter to a teacher. You can use your own thoughts and experiences to model for students how a reader makes connections to a selection.

Here are some ideas and topics you might suggest to help students connect to *Dear Mr. Blueberry*:
• a favorite animal
• a time they were worried about an animal
• a helpful teacher
• letters they've written
• what else they know about whales, oceans, or ponds

A f t e r   R e a d i n g

DISCUSSING THE LITERATURE

Talk with students to help assess their comprehension of the story and their ability to connect to their reading by asking questions such as:

1. Do you know anyone like Emily or Mr. Blueberry? (*Possible: Mr. Blueberry reminds me of my grandpa. He knows a lot about whales, too.*)
2. Why does Emily pour salt into the pond? (*She wants to turn it into salt water.*)
3. Do you like that the story is told through letters between Emily and Mr. Blueberry? Why or why not? (*Possible: Yes, because it makes it interesting to read.*)

REREADING

After they have finished reading the selection, ask volunteers to share the connections they made in the margins. Encourage students to reread the story and write one or two new connections.

See **Comprehension** on page 196 for more help.

W r i t i n g

QUICK ASSESS

Do students' opinions:

✓ include two reasons as support?

✓ use details from the story?

✓ use capital letters and periods correctly?

In this lesson, students connect the story to their own lives and react to it. Finally, they use their notes to write a book review of the story.

WRITING ACTIVITIES

1. Making Connections

Students begin to respond to the selection by describing how the story is like something in their lives.

Sample Response:

My first-grade teacher wrote me a letter over summer vacation.

2. Expressing an Opinion

Students write their opinion of *Dear Mr. Blueberry*.

Sample Response:

I didn't think the plot was interesting.

3. Writing a Book Review

Students mark whether they liked the story or not. Then they list two reasons why they did or didn't like it.

Sample Response:

No, I did not like it. I did not like reading just letters. Plus, I do not think Emily is too smart if she thinks a whale can live in her pond!

See **Writing** on page 197 for more help.

WRITING REMINDERS

As students explain their opinions, remind them to:

• Include two reasons to support their opinion.
• Use complete sentences.
• Be sure to use correct punctuation.

Vocabulary

WORDS FROM THE SELECTION

Directions: Read each sentence. Then say what you think the underlined words mean.

1. "I love whales very much and I think I saw one in my <u>pond</u> today."

I think <u>pond</u> means _____.

2. "Please send me some <u>information</u> on whales, as I think he might be hurt."

I think <u>information</u> means _____.

3. "Here are some <u>details</u> about whales."

I think <u>details</u> means _____.

4. "Yours <u>sincerely</u> Your teacher, Mr. Blueberry"

I think <u>sincerely</u> means _____.

5. "I'm sure your parents won't be <u>pleased</u>"

I think <u>pleased</u> means _____.

Comprehension

RESPONDING TO A READING

Directions: Read the sentence starters. Fill in the rest of the sentence with your ideas about the story.

1. I think Emily is _____ because

_____.

2. Mr. Blueberry reminds me of _____

because_____

_____.

3. The best part of the story was_____

because_____

_____.

4. I would tell my friends to read/not read this book because

_____

_____.

Writing

CAPITAL LETTERS AND PERIODS

Directions: In each sentence below, there is 1 error. Either a capital letter or a period is missing. Add what is needed.

1. Emily thinks she has a whale in her pond

2. mr. Blueberry helps Emily.

3. Mr. Blueberry knows a lot about whales

4. Mr. blueberry is Emily's teacher.

WRITING

Directions: Write a sentence about Emily. Tell what you know about her.

_____

_____

_____

_____

3   What's It All Mean?

B e f o r e | *R e a d i n g*

FOCUS
As you read, ask yourself, "What is the author trying to say to me?"

In this lesson, students learn how to determine the author's message.

BUILDING BACKGROUND

1. Vocabulary

To help students with the selection's vocabulary, ask them to complete these **Cloze Sentences**. To begin, ask a volunteer to read a sentence with the correct vocabulary word added. After completing the activity, have students make up new sentences using these words for other students to complete:

   edge   shadow   lifted   hooted   pumped

1. "Then the owl (*pumped*) its great wings and lifted off the branch like a shadow without sound."
2. "The shadow (*hooted*) again."
3. "The owl's call came closer, from high up in the trees on the (*edge*) of the meadow."
4. "But I was a (*shadow*) as we walked home."
5. "All of a sudden an owl shadow, part of the big tree shadow, (*lifted*) off and flew right over us."

See **Vocabulary** on page 201 for more practice with these words.

2. Prereading

Use this **Think-Pair-and-Share** activity to get students ready to read the story. Ask students to read these sentences from the story and then predict what it will be about.
1. "Nothing in the meadow moved."
2. "We watched silently with heat in our mouths, the heat of all those words we had not spoken."
3. "Pa turned on his big flashlight and caught the owl just as it was landing on a branch."
4. "It flew back into the forest."
5. " 'Time to go home,' Pa said to me."

ADDITIONAL READING

Additional selections by Jane Yolen include:
The Firebird (HarperCollins, 2002)
How Do Dinosaurs Say Goodnight? (Scholastic, 2000)
All the Secrets of the World (Little, Brown and Company, 1991)

D u r i n g | *R e a d i n g*

FOCUS ON SKILLS

1. Active Reading

Students are asked to write what they think the author is trying to tell them.
Sample Response:
Owls are special animals.

2. Critical Reading Focus

In this lesson, students explore the importance of understanding an author's message. The ability to identify what the author has to say about a subject will enable students to better understand what the story is all about and remember its key parts.

D u r i n g R e a d i n g

FOCUS ON THE SELECTION
Focus on key passages in the selection to help students see how they can recognize what the author has to say about a subject.

from *Owl Moon*
by Jane Yolen

Ask students,"What do you think Jane Yolen is trying to tell you about owls?"

Page 100

All of a sudden an owl shadow, part of the big tree shadow, lifted off and flew right over us.

Talk about the meaning of this paragraph. Ask students, "What does the phrase 'the heat of all those words we had not spoken' mean?"

Page 101

We watched silently with heat in our mouths, the heat of all those words we had not spoken.

Ask students,"What do you think Jane Yolen is trying to tell you about how the narrator and Pa feel about owls?"

For one minute, three minutes, maybe even a hundred minutes, we stared at one another.

Make clear that by using certain phrases (such as,"like a shadow without sound") Jane Yolen is letting her readers know that she thinks owls are mysterious, amazing animals.

Page 102

Then the owl pumped its great wings and lifted off the branch like a shadow without sound.

Ask students,"What is Jane Yolen trying to tell you here?" Help students realize how much the girl and her father must have hoped they would see an owl that night.

Page 103

The kind of hope that flies on silent wings under a shining Owl Moon.

As you walk students through these parts of the reading, be sure that they are following what's happening. Have them share their feelings about what the owls do and about what the girl and her father are like. You may want to have students spend a few minutes looking at the picture on page 103 and discussing what an "Owl Moon" might mean.

A f t e r R e a d i n g

DISCUSSING THE LITERATURE
Talk with students to help assess their comprehension and understanding of the story by asking questions such as:
1. What did you learn about owls from this story? (*Possible: I learned that owls can move very quietly.*)
2. Tell how you think Jane Yolen feels about owls. (*Possible: I think she likes them. I can tell by the words she uses to describe them.*)
3. What did you like best about this story? (*Possible: I liked the ending when the girl and her dad were walking home under the Owl Moon.*)

REREADING
After students have finished reading the selection, have them return to the story to find other places where Yolen gives hints about what her message might be.

See **Comprehension** on page 202 for more help.

W r i t i n g

QUICK ASSESS
Do students' stories:

✔ have a clear beginning, middle, and end?

✔ create a clear picture of the animal?

✔ show creativity?

In this lesson, students first tell what two key sentences from the story mean to them, and then they write their own story about an animal.

WRITING ACTIVITIES

1. What It Means
Students begin to respond to the selection by describing what two sentences from *Owl Moon* mean to them.
Sample Response:

> This sentence makes me feel like I can see the owl taking off from the branch.

2. Writing an Animal Story
Students continue responding to the selection by writing a story about an animal.
Sample Response:

> Once upon a time there was a beautiful horse named Missy. She lived in a big barn. Missy had black hair with a few white spots. She was so pretty. I loved to ride her. She was a gentle horse. One day we went riding. Missy got scared of something and started going too fast. I fell off and hurt my leg. Missy stopped running and came back to stay with me. Soon I felt better. I got back on Missy, and we walked slowly back to the barn.

See **Writing** on page 203 for more help.

WRITING REMINDERS
As students write their stories, remind them to:
- Tell what happens in the beginning, middle, and end.
- Give details about the animal.
- Include a title.

Vocabulary

WORDS FROM THE SELECTION

Directions: Use the words in the word box to fill in the blanks.

edge	shadow	lifted	hooted	pumped

What I Learned from *Owl Moon*

A girl and her dad went looking for owls. They hear the owl

from the _____ of the meadow. The owl

_____. It _____ its wings

and _____ off the tree. The girl felt like a

_____ when she walked home.

WORD STUDY: Prefixes and Suffixes

Directions: Add a prefix or suffix to each of these words.

New Word

1. friend + *-ly* = _____

2. *un-* + happy = _____

3. help + *-er* = _____

Comprehension

MAKING A STORYBOARD

Directions: Retell what happens in *Owl Moon*. Draw pictures of the action. Write a label below each picture.

1.

2.

3.

4.

Writing

SPELLING

Directions: Can you find the 6 spelling mistakes in this story? Circle each word that isn't spelled correctly.

My ant and eye went four a walk. We saw a big owl. My aunt screamed. Then we saw a brown dear. I thik the deer could here us because it ran away.

REWRITING A STORY

Directions: Rewrite the story with all the words spelled correctly.

_____

_____

_____

_____

_____

_____

_____

_____

_____

_____

_____

_____

Acknowledgments

78, 79, 82 "Tuesday's Lunch" from *Fox All Week* by Edward Marshall, pictures by James Marshall, copyright © 1984 by Edward Marshall, text. Used by permission of Dial Books for Young Readers, an imprint of Penguin Putnam Books for Young Readers, a division of Penguin Putnam Inc. All rights reserved.

20, 23–25, 36–38, 41, 86–88 "Growing Up" from *More Tales of Amanda Pig* by Jean Van Leeuwen, pictures by Ann Schweninger, copyright © 1985 by Jean Van Leeuwen, text. Used by permission of Dial Books for Young Readers, an imprint of Penguin Putnam Books for Young Readers, a division of Penguin Putnam Inc. All rights reserved.

93 From *Henry and Mudge Under the Yellow Moon* by Cynthia Rylant. Reprinted with the permission of Simon & Schuster Books for Young Readers, an imprint of Simon & Schuster Children's Publishing Division from *Henry and Mudge Under the Yellow Moon* by Cynthia Rylant. Text copyright © 1987 Cynthia Rylant.

98, 99 "The Scary Movie" from *The Adventures of Sugar and Junior* by Angela Shelf Medearis. Text copyright © 1995 by Angela Shelf Medearis. All rights reserved. Reprinted from *The Adventures of Sugar and Junior* by permission of Holiday House, Inc.

107, 109 From *The Sun Is Always Shining Somewhere* by Allan Fowler. Copyright © 1991 by Children's Press, Inc.

113 From *Germs Make Me Sick!* By Melvin Berger. Text Copyright © 1985, 1995 by Melvin Berger. Used by permission of HarperCollins Publishers.

118, 119 From *Sleep Is For Everyone* by Paul Showers. Text Copyright © 1974 by Paul Showers. Used by permission of HarperCollins Publishers.

126, 127, 130, 131 *Jamal's Busy Day,* written by Wade Hudson, illustrated by George Ford and © 1994 by Just Us Books, Inc. Reprinted by permission of the publisher.

132, 133, 136 From *Truman's Aunt Farm* by Jama Kim Kattigan. Text copyright © 1994 by Jama Kattigan. Reprinted by permission of Houghton Mifflin Company. All rights reserved.

139, 141 "The Wishing Well" from *Mouse Tales* by Arnold Lobel. Copyright © 1972 by Arnold Lobel. Used by permission of HarperCollins Publishers.

146, 147, 149 "Changing" from *The Llama Who Had No Pajama: 100 Favorite Poems*, copyright © 1981 Mary Ann Hoberman, reprinted by permission of Harcourt, Inc.

153, 155, 157 "Jeannie Had a Giggle" from *Brown Angels: An Album of Pictures and Verse* by Walter Dean Myers. Copyright © 1993 by Walter Dean Myers. Used by permission of HarperCollins Publishers.

159, 162 "Big Plans" from *Danitra Brown Leaves Town* by Nikki Grimes. Copyright © 2002 by Nikki Grimes. Used by permission of HarperCollins Publishers.

167 From *The Elephant* by Paula Z. Hogan. © Steck-Vaughn Company. All rights reserved. Reprinted with permission from Steck-Vaughn Company, Austin, Texas.

172, 173 From *The Alligator* by Sabrina Crewe. © Steck-Vaughn Company. All rights reserved. Reprinted with permission from Steck-Vaughn Company, Austin, Texas.

178, 179, 181 From *Pop! A Book About Bubbles* by Kimberly Brubaker Bradley. Copyright © 2001 by Kimberly Brubaker Bradley. Used by permission of HarperCollins Publishers.

Skill	Teacher's Guide	Student Edition
Anticipation Guide	98, 112, 166	
Ask Questions	78, 98, 126, 186	10, 12, 24, 42, 88
Character	86, 126	14, 42
Cloze Sentences	86, 118, 152, 198	
Connect	192	96
Context Clues	78, 98, 132, 172	
Main Idea	106, 112	30, 34
Mark Up the Text	78, 92, 106, 112, 132, 146	8, 12, 20, 30, 34, 47, 60
Matching Definitions	92, 126	
Message	118, 166, 198	38, 72, 100
Plot	98	24
Predict	78	9, 12
Preview	78, 92, 106, 118, 132, 152, 172, 186	
Problem	138, 186	53, 88
Retell	118, 172	38
Rhyme	146	60
Rhyme String	146	
Sensory Details	152, 158	63, 66
Sequence	172	77
Setting	92	20
Think-Pair-and-Share	86, 126, 146, 178, 198	
Topic	198	82
Underline	86, 166, 178	14, 72, 82
Visualize	78, 138, 158	11, 12, 53, 66
Vocabulary Inventory	112, 158, 178	
Vocabulary Quiz Show	106, 138, 166, 192	
Word Choice	132	47, 63, 66
Word Web	138, 158, 192	